Revolution at Queen's Park

Essays on Governing Ontario

Edited by Sid Noel

James Lorimer & Company, Publishers
Toronto, 1997

James Lorimer & Company Ltd. acknowledges the support of the Department of Canadian Heritage and the Ontario Arts Council in the development of writing and publishing in Canada. We acknowledge the support of the Canada Council for the Arts for our publishing program.

Cover illustration: Frank Edwards

Canadian Cataloguing in Publication Data

Revolution at Queen's Park: essays on governing Ontario

Includes index.

ISBN 1-55028-547-5 (bound) ISBN 1-55028-546-7 (pbk.)
1. Ontario. Legislative Assembly - Elections, 1995
2. Ontario. Politics and government - 1990-1995. *
3. Ontario. Politics and government - 1995- .*
4. Noel, S.J.R. (Sidney John Roderick), 1938- .

FC3077.2.R48 1997   971.3'04   C97-930942-5
F1058.R48 1997

James Lorimer & Company Ltd., Publishers
35 Britain Street
Toronto, Ontario
M5A 1R7

Printed and bound in Canada

Contents

List of Figures and Tables

Preface

In the June 1995 Ontario election, the resurgent Progressive Conservatives under the leadership of Mike Harris swept to victory, winning eighty-two of one hundred and thirty seats and forming a majority government. This outcome surprised most electoral observers: in the previous election in 1990 the PCs had finished a distant third, winning a mere twenty seats compared to seventy-four for the New Democrats and thirty-six for the Liberals. In addition, they had trailed the Liberals by a wide margin in public opinion polls until a few weeks before election day.

The PC victory marked the third change of government in Ontario in little more than a decade — a decade that saw each of the three major parties decisively defeated in turn. The 1995 election was also the second in a row in which the front-running party had been overtaken in the late stages of the campaign by a party which, when the campaign began, was far behind in the opinion polls and seemingly had little chance of winning. The magnitude of the turnaround was also striking: no fewer than nineteen ridings elected PC members for the first time in at least twenty years, and in some cases for the first time in thirty or forty years.

The election of the Harris Conservatives, and the radical agenda they have pursued since taking office, call into question some long-standing assumptions about the nature of Ontario society and politics. The old assumptions about Ontario's inherent social stability and political moderation, for example, seem no longer to hold and it is plainly no longer true that the province can only be governed from the middle or that a centrist "progressive conservatism" is the only recipe for political success. One consequence has been a sharply heightened awareness on the part of Ontarians — who have generally been the most federally oriented of Canadians — of the vital role that Queen's Park plays in their daily lives. The magnitude and ideological direction of the changes taking place in Ontario have also touched off a lively and wide-ranging debate in the universities, the media, and among the public.

In the following chapters, eight authors with a special interest in Ontario explore various aspects and implications of the shift to Tory rule, the economic and political context in which the shift occurred, and its potential long-term significance.

In Chapter 1, I review the state of the Tory revolution at approximately its mid-point, with particular attention to the Toronto megacity and government restructuring issues. In Chapter 2, A. Brian Tanguay analyses the record of the preceding NDP government and its part in creating the circumstances that led to the PC victory in 1995. In Chapter 3, Peter Woolstencroft reflects on the impact of the past decade on Ontario's political culture and assesses the province's likely future in an era of growing globalization and reduced state power. In Chapter 4, John Wilson examines Ontario's recent electoral past and the performances of its parties and leaders, placing its seemingly wild swings in the broad context of history. In Chapter 5, Robert MacDermid presents the findings of his research on the parties' television advertising strategies, in an election in which television was, more than ever before, the overwhelmingly dominant medium of political communication. In Chapter 6, Geoffrey E. Hale analyses Ontario's changing demographic and electoral patterns, combining census and voting data to illuminate important underlying factors in the rise of the Tory tide. In Chapter 7, Peter Dungan uses a sophisticated economic forecasting model to assess Ontario's (and Canada's) economic outlook for the next five to ten years, upon which so much of the Harris government's agenda — and perhaps also its re-election prospects — will ultimately hinge. In Chapter 8, Graham White focuses upon the fascinating mechanics of the transition from NDP to PC rule, and the implications for the machinery of government at Queen's Park. In Chapter 9, David A. Wolfe provides an original account of the little-known but vitally important world of Queen's Park policy-making systems, based partly on his own inside experience with the Rae government.

In the preparation of this volume I have benefited from much help, which it is now my pleasure to acknowledge. I am grateful to the Political Economy Research Group and the Faculty of Social Science of the University of Western Ontario for their sponsorship of the "Governing Ontario" conference of November 1995, where the idea for this book first arose and where earlier versions of most of the chapters were originally presented as papers. My special thanks to Ron Wintrobe and Bob Young, co-directors of PERG, and Peter Neary, Dean of Social Science, for their generous encouragement; to Don Spanner for his assistance in organizing the conference; to Bob Williams, Jim Davies and Neil Bradford, for their thoughtful and informative commentaries on the papers; to the staff of the Social Science Computing Centre for help in reproducing the tables; to my wife, Carol Hargreaves, for her close reading of the manuscript and her many valuable suggestions; to Jim Lorimer for his support and advice; and to Diane Young for her expert editorial guidance at every stage of this project.

Sid Noel
London, Ontario, June 1997

Ontario's Tory Revolution

Sid Noel

In January 1997, less than two years after assuming power, the Progressive Conservative (PC) government of Mike Harris at a stroke removed any doubts that might have lingered about its true nature and intent. It had promised to inaugurate a "common sense revolution" in the way Ontario was governed, and during the week of January 13, 1997, (appropriately dubbed "megaweek"), it kept at least the second half of that promise, unleashing a sudden, orchestrated barrage of ministerial announcements that proposed nothing less than the root-and-branch reshaping of the province's system of government, including fundamental changes to education, municipal governance, public transit, and a broad range of social services. These announcements were followed by a series of government bills introduced in the legislature. Whether the proposed changes were the product of "common sense" or "pure folly" or "blind ideology" was, of course, hotly debated, but there was no denying their daring sweep or their revolutionary character. Even many of the government's supporters were shocked by the sheer radicalism of what was being proposed.

The Omnibus Bill

Some earlier measures of the government had also been drastic, but these could be seen — and were repeatedly portrayed by Harris and his ministers — as unavoidable actions that were necessitated by the mistakes and fiscal excesses of the preceding New Democratic Party (NDP) government. Other measures were portrayed as keeping PC party promises made during the election campaign. These included reducing the level of welfare payments and requiring able-bodied recipients to work for their benefits, reversing an NDP labour law that had banned the use of replacement workers in strikes, dismantling the NDP's employment equity program, and cancelling the use of photo radar to ticket speeders on Ontario highways.

The most prominent early measure by far — and the clearest harbinger of things to come — was the "Omnibus Bill" (Bill 26, the Savings and Restructuring Act), introduced in November 1995. Bill 26 was closely related to the government's previously announced plans to make deep cuts in public expenditures, including the laying off of some thirteen thousand public servants. Because of its Draconian intent and vast sweep, which would affect nearly fifty separate statutes, it immediately became a source of violent controversy and public protest. But the bill eventually passed (on January 30, 1996), endowing the government with the extraordinary new powers it had sought: it would now be able to cut a wide swath through the whole fabric of Ontario public policy.

Among the act's multifold sections were provisions that gave the government unilateral power to close or merge hospitals, determine where doctors would be allowed to practise, impose road tolls and a wide range of new user fees for "consumers" of government services, reduce environmental protection safeguards and corporate clean-up requirements, and deregulate the price of prescription drugs under the Ontario drug benefit plan. In addition, the bill authorized the municipalities to dissolve conservation authorities, health boards, and other such bodies and impose numerous new tolls, service charges, and user fees — sources of revenue the municipalities would soon need to meet new responsibilities the province was about to download upon them.

None of these measures, however, was as dramatic or as revolutionary as the megaweek proposals. Although the earlier measures aimed to make changes — often radical changes — to existing policies and practices, they nevertheless left the structures of government largely unaffected. A future government might therefore choose to reverse the PCs' initiatives, just as the PCs had reversed the NDP's.

Megaweek

By contrast, the megaweek proposals' aim was to bring about fundamental change in the historic, bedrock institutions of the province — change that would eventually alter the very nature of Ontario's political life. The rationale for the proposals, moreover, was plainly ideological: what lay behind them, only thinly veiled by claims of fiscal necessity, was a vision of a new Ontario — an Ontario where people would be less reliant on government, or, at any rate, where they would have less government to rely on. The new Ontario would be more cheaply and efficiently governed, more responsive to market forces, and generally more individualistic and competitive than the old. Finally, the changes proposed would be so costly to reverse that it would be practically impossible for any future government to reverse them.

In effect, the Harris government was proposing not to renovate Ontario's large and sprawling governmental house, but rather to bulldoze it and build a new and smaller structure according to its own blueprint. In the process, the age-old questions of "who does what?" and "who pays for what?" would be given new answers — answers that would directly affect the lives of nearly all of Ontario's eleven million people.

Two key elements of the megaweek proposals were closely related and together amounted to a redefinition of the roles and financial responsibilities of the province and its municipalities. First, in a move so bold and far-reaching that it seemed to catch municipal politicians and officials totally off guard, the Harris government proposed to take over the entire cost of funding education, thereby shifting responsibility for $5.4 billion of expenditure from municipal property taxes to the province's general revenue. It also proposed (in Bill 104, the Fewer School Boards Act) to cut the number of school boards from 129 to 66 and the number of school trustees from 1900 to 700. The same bill placed a ceiling of $5,000 on trustees' salaries (which had previously ranged as high as $48,000), for a projected saving of $150 million annually. The second key element in the government's plan was equally drastic. As a trade-off for the shift in education funding, major new responsibilities for the funding of social welfare, public housing, transit, long-term health care, and a variety of other essential and costly public services previously funded by the province would be wholly or partially downloaded onto the municipalities and hence onto the residential property tax rolls.

The Toronto Megacity Issue

In Toronto, megaweek followed fast on the heels of an earlier shock: the Harris government's introduction in December of Bill 103, the City of Toronto Act, a sweeping measure designed both to amalgamate Metro Toronto's six municipalities into a single "megacity" and recast its system of government.[1] This measure, even more than the restructuring plan, seemed to come straight "out of the blue." There had been no hint of it in the PC party's 1995 election platform, the Common Sense Revolution. Moreover, it ran directly counter to the 1996 Report of the Greater Toronto Area (GTA) Task Force which had recommended *strengthening* the lower tier of municipal government and establishing a new regional government that would encompass the whole of the GTA, not just Metropolitan Toronto.[2] The GTA Task Force, however, had been appointed under the NDP government.

In effect, Bill 103 would *abolish* Toronto's lower tier of municipal government, which historically had been based on cities and boroughs and replace it with a single citywide council made up of a directly elected mayor and forty-four councillors. These would replace the existing system's 106 municipal officials. As if to emphasize the revolutionary intent of the legislation, the new councillors would not represent any recognizable local communities; instead, their new wards would be based on the city's twenty-two federal electoral ridings (which would also become new provincial ridings under Bill 81, the Fewer Politicians Act).

Provincewide financial restructuring and the Toronto megacity proposal were separate issues, but coming so close together, they were seen by many Torontonians as a package deal — a "double whammy" whose combined impact would be hugely damaging to their local communities and costly to their pocketbooks. The result was an upsurge of civic discontent that was soon channelled into anti-amalgamation protest meetings. These were organized by Citizens for Local Democracy, a new grass-roots movement that quickly became a thorn in the government's side. Its meetings attracted large and noisily defiant crowds, reawakening the city's sense of civic pride and reviving its tradition of local activism. Equally important, it attracted massive media attention. Toronto is a media-saturated city, and its media tend to be intensely Toronto-centric; this tendency was something that the Harris government was slow to grasp but that its opponents understood perfectly and exploited brilliantly. Citizens for Local Democracy excelled in the staging of political theatre — a form of politics that television naturally finds captivating — such as the Rebellion of '97 Parade, in which thousands of marchers from across the city took part in a political pageant that mixed local politicians with musicians and entertainers, including a float carrying a costumed actor playing the part of William Lyon Mackenzie,

Toronto's first mayor and a famous rebel whose failed 1837 march on Toronto was nominally the parade's inspiration. The movement also featured the active participation of celebrities, including novelist Margaret Atwood. Its leading media spokesperson was former mayor John Sewell, a well-known urban activist with extensive political and media experience.

A Tory-connected countergroup, the Alliance for Amalgamation, was belatedly assembled to sponsor pro-amalgamation meetings and media advertisements, but its efforts proved ineffectual. By the time it entered the fray, in late February, the opposition movement had already won the battle for public opinion: polls showed more than two-thirds of Metro residents opposed to amalgamation, and on March 3, when plebiscites were held in the six Toronto municipalities, amalgamation was opposed by 76.1 per cent of voters.

The anti-amalgamation movement, however, had won a pyrrhic victory. The turnout in the municipal plebiscites was 31.2 per cent, which was too low to confer much authority on the result; moreover, the government had announced in advance that it would not be bound by plebiscites that it had not authorized and whose bona fides it regarded as suspect. After one last piece of political theatre — an opposition filibuster in the legislature that involved voting on thousands of computer-generated amendments — Bill 103 was passed into law with only a few minor changes. In the final version of the act the number of councillors was increased from forty-four to fifty-six, and ward boundaries were redrawn to correspond to existing Metro wards rather than federal ridings, as originally proposed. The implementation of the new system would be overseen by a provincially appointed six-member transition team headed by current Metro chair Alan Tonks, a Liberal who had earlier been an opponent of amalgamation.

For the most part, however, the opposing sides were unreconciled. "That's literally the end of democracy," said John Sewell. "This is a new day, a new beginning for all of us," Municipal Affairs minister Al Leach hopefully intoned. What the passage of Bill 103 shows, concluded Liberal leader Dalton McGuinty, is "sledgehammer democracy at its worst."[3]

The anti-amalgamation campaign — despite its success in mobilizing popular opposition and attracting media attention — was, in the end, clearly no match for the Harris government. Committed to a radical agenda, less than halfway into its term, and backed by solid majority support in the legislature, the government was not about to be pressured into a humiliating political surrender. Yet that was exactly what the leaders of the anti-amalgamation movement set as their ultimate, and indeed only, objective. Since there could therefore be no basis for any low-key engagement with the government over specific aspects of amalgamation, the confrontation very quickly became personal, extreme, and rhetorical. At one point, after being hounded from meeting to meeting by a hyperbolically offensive (and repetitive) anti-amalgamation orator, Al Leach deadpanned: "That's two nights in a row this man has compared me to Hitler and that's two nights in a row that I won't respond."[4]

To have had any realistic hope of forcing the government to back down, the anti-amalgamation movement would have needed massive provincewide support, but its exclusive focus on Toronto separated it — both symbolically and politically — from many of its potential allies. It would also have had to build a wider coalition within Toronto, particularly among the city's business élite, who generally supported amalgamation but were opposed to financial restructuring (or downloading). The latter was a key "bridge" issue that the leaders of the anti-amalgamation movement failed to exploit sufficiently. Their Toronto-centric "all or nothing" strategy produced some extraordinary political theatre, but it also demonstrated, in textbook fashion, how such a strategy practically ensured that the end result would be "nothing."

The Restructuring Issue

The course taken by opponents of the government's restructuring plan stands in contrast to the course taken by opponents of the Toronto megacity. When first announced, the government's restructuring plan was so startling it overshadowed all other issues, including the megacity, and it garnered little public or media support. The response of the province's large cities was uniformly negative, for reasons that are not hard to fathom. The new system would produce a radically different pattern of winners and losers — and the biggest losers of all would be the cities, with Metro Toronto losing the most. As home to 22 per cent of the Ontario population, Metro depends on a vast public transit system and contains a disproportionate share of the province's public housing (45 per cent) and welfare cases (38 per cent). Metro residents would see their tax bills soar as the city struggled to meet an estimated $378.6 million in new costs. At the same time, on the education side of the equation, they would see their well-funded public school systems reduced to the provincial average.

"I think it's like the city has been bombed," Toronto's mayor Barbara Hall declared.[5] A letter-writer to the *Globe and Mail* observed that Edvard Munch's famous painting *The Scream* was on exhibition at the Art Gallery of Ontario and "expresses our sentiments exactly."

Outside the large cities, however, reactions were generally more muted. It was not long before some rural and small-town support for the government's plan began to surface, usually from those who had worked through the numbers and found that it was not their municipal ox that was going to be gored. But on the whole there was a notable lack of enthusiasm, even among the supposed beneficiaries, for it took no great prescience to see that the projected benefits might well turn out to be illusory.

In the field of education, for example, the elimination of dependency on a local tax base would ostensibly benefit underfunded rural and Catholic school boards and suburban municipalities in which a large population of young families live and education accounts for a high proportion of property taxes (for example, 72 per cent in Vaughan compared to 55 per cent in Toronto). But any real benefit would vanish if total spending on education were cut (as also seemed to be the government's intent). Getting an equal slice of a smaller pie, in other words, might well leave the poorer school boards worse off than before. There was also widespread resentment over the government's plan to appoint an "Education Improvement Commission" with the power to override the decisions of elected school boards. "This violates everything held dear in a democracy," London trustee Peter Jaffe protested. "With something this radical, why was there no consultation, no analysis of the impact?"[6]

In the field of social services, rural and suburban municipalities — with their disproportionately low number of welfare cases, minimal public transit, and absence of public housing — would again appear to be the clear winners. But education costs in these areas are likely to decline in the long run, barring a sudden increase in the birth rate, while their social service costs are likely to increase, and their welfare costs are unpredictable. Rural poverty is not unknown in Ontario, and the number of rural welfare cases could rise sharply if hard-pressed cities ceased to provide welfare services for new migrants. Even normally affluent suburban communities are not immune from sudden increases in economic and social distress following plant-closings or lay-offs. Hence, when Community Services minister Janet Ecker chose to make her megaweek announcement in the Town of Oakville (one of Ontario's richest communities, whose officials might have been expected to applaud the prospect of lower property taxes), she was not exactly greeted with an outpouring of gratitude. The response of Oakville mayor Ann Mulvale was succinct: "It may not impact on us for a few years, but we know that if there is another economic downturn, we could be badly hurt."[7]

Ignoring the near-unanimous analysis of both experienced local officials and academic experts on municipal finance, Al Leach doggedly insisted that the government's plan was designed to be "revenue neutral" as it included a $1 billion annual "Community Reinvestment Fund" to help cover any shortfall in municipal revenues and a further $800 million in "transitional" grants over four years. And if any municipality still ended up short, he added, its politicians should simply cut expenses or "they shouldn't bother running for election."[8]

Running for election, indeed, was obviously not far from the minds of any of the main protagonists. With a solid forty-eight seat majority in the legislature, the government was assured of securing passage of its restructuring plan. But it also knew that, ultimately, the battle for the plan would not be won or lost in the legislature. Rather, it would be won or lost in county council chambers and city halls across the province and in the media.

The Restructuring Compromise

In the council chambers, it would be a battle for the support of Ontario's influential local government élites — municipal politicians and administrators who would be largely responsible for the plan's implementation and whose cooperation was essential. Almost unnoticed amid the sound and fury of the Toronto megacity fight, their opposition to the plan's financial downloading provisions had been quietly building steam. The organization that represents their interests is the Association of Municipalities of Ontario (AMO). By mid-March it had forged a broad consensus among its membership, which includes both large and small municipalities, and brought sufficient pressure to bear upon the Harris government to get virtually the whole plan reopened for discussion. This in itself was a substantial victory, for it amounted to a tacit acknowledgement by the government that its original proposals were deeply flawed and in need of rethinking. Mike Harris, in his inimitable fashion, expressed the government's new-found flexibility: "Other than a whole bunch of negative nabobbers who want the status quo, nothing is a non-starter."[9]

The AMO's strategy from the beginning was to draw the government into closed-door negotiations rather than to demand that it publicly wave a white flag and surrender. Now, with Harris's go-ahead and a firm agreement to negotiate, it was in a position to obtain substantial concessions. Two AMO negotiating teams were set up to develop alternative proposals to present to the government: one team was to deal with social issues, the other with financial and transition issues. Both teams were chaired by AMO president Terry Mundell, both included members drawn from large and small municipalities, and both included local politicians with known ties to the Harris Tories.

By the end of April, the AMO and the government had struck a compromise agreement that was subsequently endorsed in the provincial budget of May 6. Largely through the AMO's efforts, that agreement had the support of an impressive array of organizations and individuals, including separate- and public-school trustees and the representatives of large and small municipalities. In essence, the government moved a long way on the specifics of its restructuring plan but did not yield on its original purpose of capping expenditures. As Al Leach put it, "the size of the pot had to remain the same, but if we could mix the ingredients a little differently to come up with the same answer, we would do that."[10] The final mix of ingredients, however, was significantly different from the original mix. Among the key new provisions were the following: the municipalities would continue to pay 20 per cent of welfare costs instead of the 50 per cent originally proposed, but the total bill for these costs would be bigger, since the municipalities would in addition have to assume responsibility for a similar share of family benefits, which had previously been funded entirely by the province; the education tax would not be removed from residential properties but instead would be reduced by 50 per cent; and the municipalities would assume responsibility for the costs and administration of social housing, though financial sweeteners would make the transfer more palatable.

The AMO's success stands in sharp contrast to the failure of the anti-amalgamation movement in Toronto and may be explained by three factors. First, the AMO leaders were accustomed to dealing with Queen's Park and had a realistic understanding of what was politically possible; their strategy was to negotiate piecemeal concessions, not to engage in a pitched battle with the government.

Second, they kept themselves out of the media spotlight, preferring instead the occasional controlled briefing of the press; AMO president Terry Mundell, the politically astute Reeve of Erin, built a formidable coalition of support while remaining virtually unknown to the television cameras. Third, the government's intransigence in the Toronto megacity struggle in Toronto eventually worked to the AMO's advantage; once that battle was won, the government moved quickly on the restructuring plan and seemed anxious to reach a settlement with the municipalities that would make it appear reasonable and accommodating.

The Media Blitz

The Harris government was apparently well aware from the beginning of megaweek that it would be engaged in a battle for control of the media spin, and ultimately for control of the political agenda in the lead-up to the next election, and it prepared its strategy accordingly. In a move unprecedented for an Ontario government in mid-term, the megaweek announcements were accompanied by an advertising blitz that was unabashedly partisan in nature, with a portion of it indeed paid for by the PC party. A portion that was not — a pamphlet promoting the benefits of a Toronto megacity — was ruled by the Speaker of the Legislative Assembly to be in contempt, since it treated the proposed amalgamation as a done deed, ignoring the fact that the requisite legislation had not been passed. This conveyed the impression, said the Speaker, that "the legislature had a pro forma, tangential, even inferior role in the legislative and law-making process."[11] The government was pilloried by the opposition and perhaps momentarily embarrassed, but, however deplorable, the episode was also revealing: the offending pamphlet's assumption that the legislature lacked any real importance was not inaccurate, for there was no doubt that Bill 103 would eventually be passed. The government, moreover, had already clearly signalled that it regarded the legislature's role as secondary: its preferred forum for unveiling its megaweek plan had not been the legislature but rather the staged ministerial announcement — in time for the six o'clock television news. The government's medium of choice for its advertising blitz was also television — where the content and style of its ads, and its ad-placement strategy, reflected the same obvious professional touch that the PC party's communications advisers had demonstrated in the 1995 election campaign.

The main point of the ads was to portray Premier Mike Harris as a confidence-inspiring and reassuring figure. In one ad, he appears casually dressed, speaking with a soft musical accompaniment, against a moving backdrop of out-of-focus, almost subliminal images of a hockey game. His message is upbeat and direct, extolling his government's record of tax reductions and spending cuts ("The sacrifices we make today will guarantee a better future for all of us"). Another ad opens with an eye-catching visual showing an antiquated electrical system in which tangled wires burn, sputter, and short-circuit (an obvious metaphor for Ontario's government), quickly followed by a shot of a modern system of orderly, colour-coded conduits. Mike Harris then appears in business attire, flicks the switch controlling the new system, and the set is bathed in light (the Harris plan at work).

The first postblitz opinion polls gave the ad-makers ample reason to be satisfied with their artistry, for the outpouring of protest that had greeted the megaweek proposals had evidently made no immediate dent in the Harris government's continuing popularity with the public. Indeed, the reported level of support for the Tories had actually increased, from 43 to 47 per cent, and their overall approval rating remained unusually high — above 50 per cent even in Toronto, the supposed epicentre of opposition. Later polls, however, revealed some slippage in these numbers, with the Harris government slightly trailing the opposition Liberals under their new leader, Dalton McGuinty. Nevertheless, the Harrisites remained more popular than is usual for governments at midterm and well within striking range of a repeat victory in the next election.

Ontario's Political Culture

The events of early 1997 need to be understood in the context of Ontario's fiercely competitive, exceedingly volatile electoral politics and, more generally, in the context of the province's political culture — that is, within the historic pattern of ideas, norms, and expectations concerning government that the people of Ontario hold and that broadly conditions their political behaviour.[12]

Between 1985 and 1995 Ontario ran through a series of governments, going from PC to Liberal to NDP and, in 1995, back to the PCs again. But the apparent circularity of this electoral merry-go-round is deceiving; the Ontario of 1995 was in many respects a different place from the Ontario of 1985. In the intervening decade Ontarians saw their industrial economy shaken by the impacts of globalization and continental integration; they saw unemployment reach its highest level since the Great Depression, with much attendant misery and social dislocation; they saw the once-secure framework of Confederation threatened by constitutional crises, to the utter distraction of their political leaders; and they themselves served as the agents and messengers of change by exercising their democratic sovereignty with unaccustomed vigour. By 1995, the bedrock formations of Ontario politics were visibly cracking along new fault lines. It now seemed a very long time since Ontario had been a byword for stable, moderate, managerial government, as exemplified by the pre-1985 Tory dynasty, whose unbroken rule had extended over more than four decades.

All three of Ontario's political parties were transformed during the turbulent period from 1985 to 1995, but none more so than the PC party. Thus, the PC party that "returned" to power in 1995 in reality bore only a marginal connection to the Tory dynasty of 1943–85. During a decade in the political wilderness the party had been recast in a radically different mould, becoming a new party in all but name — with a new ideology, a new ethos, and a new organization.

Ideologically, the new PC party had jettisoned the progressive wing of "progressive conservatism" and become a truly "conservative" party, in philosophical disposition as well as on specific issues of fiscal and social policy. Its closest affinities were with the federal Reform Party, the Klein government in Alberta, and the several very similar U.S. state Republican parties (such as the one in Michigan, under Governor John Engler), whose outlooks, policy positions, and strategies it largely echoed.[13]

In ethos, the new PC party embraced a kind of populism as a prominent part of its appeal, adopting a no-nonsense "people against government" rhetoric that its leader, Mike Harris, voiced ably and with evident conviction. In 1990, though overshadowed by the victory of the NDP, Harris's effective campaign as a populist "tax fighter" had secured the electoral base of his party and positioned it for a successful run in the next election. In 1995, the party's populist platform included a promise to submit any proposed tax increase to the people in a binding referendum.

Organizationally, the new PC party restructured from the ground up, but most significantly it installed a state-of-the-art election machine at the top that was in direct contact with the leader and that consisted of an élite of young U.S.-oriented campaign strategists, advertising and television specialists, pollsters, and consultants — a type of machine originally developed in the United States and increasingly familiar in other democracies (the Italian political scientist Angelo Panebianco identifies it as a distinctly modern creation, the "electoral-professional party").[14] In 1995, the new machine proved its worth by correctly aligning the PCs with newly emergent trends in Ontario public opinion. Among these were a distrust of politics and politicians; a rejection of policies designed to ensure employment "equity" for minorities, a suspicion that the welfare system was too generous and was being scandalously abused, and a sense of being overtaxed and overgoverned. All of these formed the basis of promises in the Harris party program, the Common Sense Revolution, and served as potent "hot button" issues in the 1995 election.

Prior to 1985, the old Tory party's pragmatic mix of progressivism and conservatism was generally seen as one of the key reasons for its extraordinary hold on political power. Though frustrating to ideologues, its lack of ideological purity, or even consistency, seemed curiously well attuned to the temper of the Ontario people, who were often characterized (for want of any better description) as possessing a "progressive conservative" political culture.[15] But in that bland characterization some nonconforming and potentially disruptive tendencies were overlooked.

Two of these tendencies had roots that stretched far back into the history of the province, though neither could be considered in the mainstream of its political culture. The first was a tendency towards militant sectionalism in politics; the second was a tendency to favour minimal government.[16] Both had lain dormant and were generally ignored for many years, but in the 1990s both developed new strains and surged to renewed prominence in Ontario's political life — a prominence they had not enjoyed since the nineteenth century.

The New Sectionalism

When sectionalism flared again in the 1980s and 1990s, it was not in forms it had assumed in the nineteenth century, namely, religious sectarianism and agrarian protest. Rather, it took the form of a proliferation of "new social movements": single-interest pressure groups that were largely (though not completely) secular and urban, but no less intransigent and no less strident in their demands than their earlier counterparts. Their rise was fuelled by a charter-inspired consciousness of rights, by growing ethnic diversity, by economic discontent, and by the failure of governments or political parties to articulate any convincing sense of the public interest. This new sectionalism also corresponded with the rise of a cadre of militant, highly politicized trade union leaders, who tended to focus their demands on Queen's Park, and an even more extreme cadre of leaders of new social movements, who were expert in the cultivation of grievances of every kind, both real and imagined. The influence of these leaders on electoral politics, however, turned out to be highly erratic. They were a factor in the success of the Liberals in 1985 and 1987, and an even bigger factor in the success of the NDP in 1990. But when the NDP government belatedly attempted to reassert the public interest — notably by its enactment in 1993 of the Social Contract — it became the particular target of their fury.[17] In 1995, a coalition of militant unions and new social movements turned on the government with a vengeance, demonizing Bob Rae for his "betrayal" and helping in no small measure to bring the Harris PCs to power.

The unions and new social movements were not, of course, supporters of the Harris government, except unwittingly, and were soon as openly hostile towards it as they had been towards the NDP. Since 1995 they have played a prominent role in labour-sponsored "days of protest" against public sector cutbacks and in other demonstrations. These efforts initially won them little sympathy from the wider public and made no apparent impact on the Harris government. Indeed, the government seemed to welcome protest demonstrations as an opportunity to be seen defending the province's general interest. The government's approach was to label all opposing groups as "special interests" and take an indiscriminate hard line against them. This approach worked well for a time, as there was little public sympathy for the groups involved. But the original protesters have since been joined in their opposition to the government by other nonmilitant groups, such as nurses and health care workers, who enjoy broad public respect and support. As a result, the Harris government's approach has begun to backfire — sometimes spectacularly. For example, Mike Harris dismissed the concerns of health care workers who were losing their jobs by comparing them to 1960s hula-hoop makers who had to find new employment when the hula-hoop craze came to an end.[18] Harris later apologized, but his memorably foolish insult is likely to echo throughout the next election campaign.

Minimal Government

In the nineteenth century, a belief in the virtue of minimal government and a corresponding tendency to deny the social utility of politics and politicians were consistent themes in the radical populism of the political left. In the 1830s, William Lyon Mackenzie was a fierce critic of the size of government, not just of its unrepresentative nature. Later in the nineteenth century, successive waves of populism swept across the border from the United States, borne by agrarian protest movements such as the Patrons and Husbandry and Patrons of Industry, which harked back to a mythical Arcadia where government scarcely existed — and where there were no politicians. By the 1890s, minimal government was also a popular idea on the right of the ideological spectrum. One of its leading advocates was Goldwin Smith, eminent Toronto professor and journalist, who, with malice aforethought, missed no opportunity to deride the Liberal government of the day for what he regarded as its grandiose pretensions. All that was necessary to govern Ontario, he maintained, was "a good practical council of reeves."[19]

A century later, Smith's views were again resonating strongly in a modern "neo-conservative" phraseology borrowed from the U.S. right. Such views were faithfully reflected in the PC party's 1995 election manifesto, the Common Sense Revolution, and were a factor in the party's victory. During megaweek, the antigovernment, antipolitician sentiments of the government were again prominently on display in its appeal to the electorate. "You have to understand," said Harris of the critics of his restructuring plan, "that a lot of these politicians and bureaucrats are going to lose their jobs, and that's unfortunate. But the fact of the matter is, we have too much government, too many politicians, too many bureaucrats."[20]

Conclusion

The PC party won power in part by successfully aligning itself with certain emergent tendencies in Ontario politics, and particularly with a rising tide of antigovernment sentiment and disillusionment with politics. But it was also the inadvertent beneficiary of other tendencies, such as the resurgence of militant interest-group sectionalism that had proven so damaging to the NDP, and of incidental factors, such as the Ontario Liberal party's inept election campaign. What remains to be seen is whether the Tory victory in the 1995 election was due mainly to recurrent political tendencies that surged powerfully for a brief time but are now receding, as historically is their pattern, or whether it was truly reflective of a profound, long-term ideological realignment, a fundamental rightward shift in the political culture of Ontario.

The Harris government is banking its future on the belief that a fundamental shift has indeed taken place. This belief underlies its entire approach to governing, which, as a result, displays an unusual degree of ideological consistency.

In 1995, Harris's no-nonsense, right-wing rhetoric and promises to cut both the size of the public sector and taxes obviously struck a responsive chord. After more than four years of economic recession and ballooning provincial deficits, many Ontario voters — and not merely fiscal conservatives — felt that the burden of the public sector had become excessive. Even the NDP government of Bob Rae had come to the same conclusion, as its ill-fated Social Contract initiative attested.

In mid-1997, however, there are signs that many Ontarians are beginning to judge the matter differently. Threatened by hospital closings, the replacement of local school boards by huge consolidated boards, the elimination of many local governments through amalgamation, and deep cuts in the staffing of environmental protection agencies, they are coming to the view that the Harris axe is cutting too deep — that the problem is fast becoming one of too little government, not too much.

The Harris government pollsters are no doubt tracking this worrisome new trend with care, and evidently to some effect. The Ontario budget of May 1997, while continuing to reduce the total level of public spending, also included a flurry of new and repackaged spending commitments that were redolent of electoral calculation. The printed version of the budget was even subtitled "Investing in the Future" and illustrated with pictures of a hospital operating theatre and of students working at classroom computers. Its unsubtle message was designed to counter a growing popular perception that valued public services, particularly in the areas of health care and education, are being needlessly sacrificed or placed in jeopardy for no reason other than to serve a doctrinaire agenda. If that perception were to take hold, it would no doubt seriously dim the Harris government's re-election prospects.

The government's options, however, are decidedly limited. It has gone too far to turn back without a massive loss of credibility and must therefore go forward. If it is correct in its belief that Ontarians will eventually appreciate the necessity and the wisdom of the Tory revolution that is its handiwork, its reward will be another victory in the next election. If it is wrong, its days are numbered.

Endnotes

1. I am grateful to Andrew Sancton for his helpful comments on an earlier draft of this chapter. For background to the mega-city issue, see his book, *Governing Canada's City-Regions*, Montreal: Institute for Research on Public Policy, 1994, 76-82.
2. *Greater Toronto: Report of the GTA Task Force*, Toronto: Publications Ontario, January 1996, 166.
3. *Globe and Mail*, April 22, 1997, A8.
4. *Toronto Star*, February 16, 1997, A11.
5. *Globe and Mail*, January 18, 1977, A8.
6. *London Free Press*, January 23, 1997, A1.
7. *Toronto Star*, January 26, 1997, F4.
8. *Globe and Mail*, January 21, 1997, A5.
9. *London Free Press*, March 22, 1997, A3.
10. *Globe and Mail*, May 2, 1997, A5.
11. *Globe and Mail*, January 23, 1997, A5.
12. For a further discussion of political culture, see Sid Noel, "The Ontario Political Culture: An Interpretation," in Graham White, ed., *The Government and Politics of Ontario*, 5th ed., Toronto: University of Toronto Press, 1997.
13. Leslie Coventry, "Campaign Strategy and the Uses of Television Political Advertising in Michigan and Ontario," unpublished Ph.D. thesis, University of Western Ontario, 1996.
14. *Political Parties: Organization and Power*, Cambridge: Cambridge University Press, 1988, 262-5.
15. Donald C. MacDonald, "Ontario's Political Culture: Conservatism with a Progressive Component," *Ontario History* 84:4, (1994): 297-317.
16. S.J.R. Noel, *Patrons, Clients, Brokers: Ontario Society and Politics, 1791-1896*, Toronto: University of Toronto Press, 1990, 298-306.
17. Thomas Walkom, *Rae Days: The Rise and Follies of the NDP*, Toronto: Key Porter, 1994, 121-46.
18. *Globe and Mail*, March 6, 1997, A1.
19. Noel, *Patrons, Clients, Brokers*, 294.
20. *London Free Press*, January 22, 1997, A1.

2

"Not in Ontario!" From the Social Contract to the Common Sense Revolution

A. Brian Tanguay

In which province did the following happen? During the election campaign, the premier-to-be mused publicly about the need to send juvenile delinquents to boot camps in order to instill in them the discipline so sadly lacking in contemporary youth, about cutting the province's overly generous welfare subsidies for people who did not work for their money, and about abolishing tenure for fat-cat professors? His party's detailed election platform promised to implement a northern version of Ronald Reagan's "voodoo economics": hefty tax cuts of 30 per cent over three years, spending cuts of 20 per cent in so-called nonpriority areas, and a balanced budget by the end of the government's mandate. After coming to power, the party set about systematically demolishing many of the previous government's legislative accomplishments, usually with no pretence of public consultation. Meanwhile, some of the new cabinet ministers distinguished themselves by their penchant for outrageous and condescending commentary: the minister of Education, a self-made millionaire and high school dropout, proposed to manufacture a crisis that would give him the pretext for radically reforming the school system along business lines. The minister of Community and Social Services, a lawyer and an amateur poet who quickly became notorious for his *bons mots* and baroque ideas, published a "menu" for people on welfare, purportedly demonstrating that it is possible for a person to survive on ninety dollars' worth of food a month and prompting one reporter to note that the nutritional value of the menu items was less than what was required for prisoners of war under the Geneva Convention.

If all of the above had taken place in the province of Alberta, with its history of right-wing populist movements and its affinity for American-style politics, then these behaviours might be considered entirely understandable. But surely this could not have taken place in staid old Ontario, which until recently had a well-deserved reputation for "political immobility."[1] Try as some of us might to close our eyes and pretend that the election of June 8, 1995, did not happen — an especially tempting reflex among those numerous pundits and academics (the present author included) who had confidently predicted at the outset of the campaign that the so-called Common Sense Revolution could not happen in Ontario — the shocking reality was that a province once noted for moderation and political stability had elected an unabashedly right-wing populist government. The electorate made this about-face only five years after installing Bob Rae and the NDP in power, and only eight years after handing David Peterson's Liberal party one of the biggest majorities in provincial political history. How can the wild fluctuations in voting behaviour in Ontario during the last decade be explained? What created the conditions for Mike Harris's remarkable sweep of the province, with his party taking eighty-two seats and 45 per cent of the popular vote, the Conservatives' highest totals since 1971?[2] And what are the implications of the Tory victory for Ontario's party system and, more generally, for the future of political parties as the primary representative institutions in liberal democracy? These are the central questions that I will seek to answer in this paper.[3]

Historical Backdrop to the 1995 Election

The various factors contributing to the remarkable longevity of the Tory dynasty in Ontario (1943–1985) have been well documented. Chief among them were the province's continuing economic prosperity during this period, despite the normal peaks and troughs of the business cycle; the ability of the Tories to revitalize themselves every ten years or so with the selection of a new leader; their successful appeal to a broad coalition of moderate voters, along with an intimidatingly efficient party organization, the vaunted "Big Blue Machine"; and, of course, the fact that opposition votes were split between two parties roughly equal in strength (at least during the 1960s and 1970s).[4]

This picture of political stasis was shattered above all by Premier Bill Davis's unilateral decision in June 1984 to extend full funding to separate schools for Grades 11 through 13. Whatever the motivation behind Davis's decision — whether to appeal to a strategically important Roman Catholic population or to "pay off" Cardinal Emmett Carter for his visible support of the Tory regime[5] — it opened up a Pandora's box of voter resentment and hostility that washed over all three political parties in the province and proved particularly harmful to Frank Miller, Davis's successor as Tory leader. The 1985 provincial election provided an eerie foreshadowing of the period that would follow the Meech Lake and Charlottetown constitutional processes, when angry voters turned against the party system as a whole and punished incumbent governments for having effectively disfranchised them. Both the NDP and the Liberals agreed with Davis's decision to fund separate schools, citing the provision concerning minority schools in the Constitution Act of 1867 as the basis for their support. All three parties studiously tried to avoid the issue during the campaign, yet voters seemed to want to talk of nothing else; all-candidates' meetings were often free-for-alls that confirmed just how strong the currents of religious animosity still were in Ontario. The Anglican Archbishop of Toronto, Lewis Garnsworthy, likened Davis to Hitler for the manner in which he had made his decision, and many voters echoed the Archbishop's sentiments.[6] This issue, combined with the lacklustre Tory campaign of 1985 and infighting among various factions of the incumbent party, laid the groundwork for the Conservatives' fall from grace. Since that time, no government has succeeded in convincing the electorate to return it to power, with the sole exception of the Liberal-NDP "coalition" of 1985–87.[7] Interestingly, severe limitations were placed on the Liberals' margin for manoeuvre during this two-year period by its minority status and formal agreement with the NDP. During the past decade, it has become increasingly apparent that many voters cherish the responsiveness and accountability of the party in power when it is in a minority situation, even if they shy away from the thought of minority government itself.

Growing voter cynicism in the late 1980s and early 1990s manifested itself in high levels of distrust of politicians, parties, and Parliament, sentiments that were amply documented first by the Spicer Report and then by the Royal Commission on Electoral Reform and Party Financing (the Lortie Commission).[8] This cynicism, combined with the shrinking economic prospects of the early 1990s, created fertile ground for sudden and dramatic shifts in the bases of party support as voters desperately sought to locate a political party that would improve their economic fortunes and, just as important, provide no-nonsense, scandal-free administration. In Ontario, voters were confronted with the additional burden of coming to terms with the declining role within the federation of their province, its deindustrializing economy, and the growing perception that other provinces were taking advantage of its financial generosity. This combination of factors translated into low tolerance among voters for governmental miscues of any kind, especially those of a venal sort, where politicians appeared to be taking advantage of their positions in power to line their pockets when many voters were simply struggling to get by.

David Peterson's Liberal government was one of the first casualties in this new climate of voter cynicism and volatility.[9] Entering the 1990 election, the Liberals were sitting at 50 per cent in the public opinion polls, and most pundits predicted a cakewalk to victory. The cakewalk, however, went disastrously awry. Voters took out their frustrations — about Meech Lake,[10] about political corruption (the Patti Starr scandal, which had tainted some of the government's top cabinet ministers and some of the premier's closest advisers), and about the deteriorating economic situation (free trade and the GST had combined to exacerbate the effects of the recession that had just started) — on the same "yuppie premier" who only months earlier had been his party's greatest asset. With under 38 per cent of the popular vote, Bob Rae and the NDP formed the first social democratic government in Ontario's history, taking seventy-four seats, thanks largely to a near-miraculous three-way split in the vote in many ridings, along with a better-than-usual showing by a welter of minor parties (see Table 1).[11]

This election result was clearly not a ringing endorsement of the NDP program, which was a thin document entitled *An Agenda for People* and which had been hastily crafted for reasons of pure political expediency by two top party advisers in the space of a weekend.[12] If social democracy were to set down roots in Canada's most populous and industrialized province, if the NDP were to have any chance of expanding its support base beyond its traditional constituencies in the public sector unions, Northern Ontario, parts of Metro Toronto, and the working-class bastions of Hamilton and Windsor, it would have to demonstrate a modicum of administrative competence and formulate credible policies through *real* consultation with the various

Table 1								
Ontario Provincial Election Results, 1943-95								
Year	Conservatives		Liberals		CCF/NDP		Other	
	Seats	% Popular Vote	Seats	% Popular Vote	Seats	% Popular Vote	Seats	% Popular Vote
1943	38	35.7	16	31.2	34	31.7	2	1.4
1945	66	44.3	14	29.8	8	22.4	2	3.5
1948	53	41.5	14	29.8	21	27.0	2	1.7
1951	79	48.5	8	31.5	2	19.1	1	0.9
1955	84	48.5	11	33.3	3	16.5	-	1.7
1959	71	46.3	22	36.6	5	16.7	-	0.4
1963	77	48.9	24	35.3	7	15.5	-	0.3
1967	69	42.3	28	31.6	20	25.9	-	0.2
1971	78	44.5	20	27.8	19	27.1	-	0.6
1975	51	36.1	36	34.3	38	28.9	-	0.7
1977	58	39.7	34	31.5	33	28.0	-	0.8
1981	70	44.4	34	33.7	21	21.1	-	0.8
1985	52.	37.0	48	37.9	25	23.8	-	1.3
1987	16	24.7	95	47.3	19	25.7	-	2.3
1990	20	23.5	36	32.4	74	37.6	-	6.5
1995	82	44.8	30	31.1	17	20.6	1	3.5

Sources: 1943–1981: Government of Ontario, Chief Election Officer, *Electoral History of Ontario: Candidates and Results, 1867–1982.*
1985–1995: Government of Ontario, Chief Election Officer, *Election Returns.*

stakeholders involved.[13] Though its defenders will argue that the Rae government was sabotaged by a neanderthal business community and a hidebound Queen's Park bureaucracy — and there is at least a measure of truth in these claims — many of its problems were self-inflicted. Thanks to its gyrations and vacillations on key economic policies, a policy style heavily tinctured with the hubris of technocrats, a tendency to engage in merely pro-forma consultation,[14] and a marked predilection for demonizing any opposition to some of its more controversial initiatives, the NDP managed in the space of five years to fritter away its miraculous mandate.[15] In the process, it sowed the seeds of a right-wing populist backlash against its brand of technocratic social engineering that would carry Mike Harris and the Conservatives to power in 1995.

The NDP in Power: The Perils of Hubris

Two defining moments occurred during the Ontario NDP's tenure in power: Floyd Laughren's first budget was unveiled on April 29, 1991, and the Social Contract (Bill 48) was imposed in June 1993.[16] The budget, in particular, had an immediate, highly negative effect on public opinion, contributing to the NDP's spectacular crash from its postelection honeymoon with the province's voters. In January 1991, 60 per cent of those surveyed had said that they would vote for the NDP if an election were held then (see Figure 1). On the first anniversary of its stunning election victory, however, voter support for the NDP stood at 36 per cent and was in freefall (see Figure 1). Of course, not all of this unpopularity can be attributed to the controversial budget; a string of embarrassing scandals, government miscues, and cabinet resignations during the party's first year in office had also played an important part in the souring of the relationship between Rae's government and the electorate.[17]

Figure 1
Ontario NDP Popularity – Poll Results, 1990–95

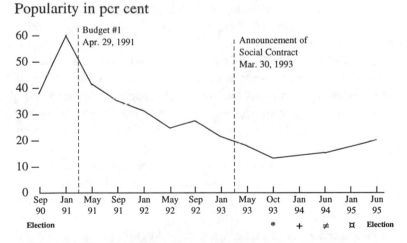

Popularity in per cent

* Environics Poll reported in *Globe & Mail* Oct. 29, 1993. Margin of error (ME) = ± 3.1%
+ Environics Poll reported in *Toronto Star* Jan. 17, 1994. ME = ± 3.1%.
≠ Angus Reid Poll reported in *Globe & Mail* June 22, 1994. ME = ± 4.5%.
¤ Environics Poll reported in *Vancouver Sun* Feb. 3, 1995. ME = n/a.

Souce (unless otherwise indicated): *The Gallup Report*, various issues. Poll results have a margin of error of ± 5.0%

In its first budget, the NDP had boldly — some would say fool-ishly — decided to swim against the tide of fiscal restraint in the rest of the country (and virtually the entire western world). Having an-nounced that his government would not fight the recession on the backs of the poor and most vulnerable, Finance Minister Floyd Laughren allowed the budget deficit to balloon to $9.7 billion, un-leashing a barrage of media commentary about the tax-happy, spend-thrift socialists at Queen's Park.[18] Even commentators normally sympathetic to the NDP noted that not a lot of job creation was purchased with the almost $10-billion deficit; more disturbingly, the government's projections wildly underestimated the depth of the recession. In *Toronto Star* journalist Thomas Walkom's estimation, the "result was the worst of all worlds — a budget Keynesian enough to anger business but not stimulative enough to do much good."[19]

Many of the economic policy reversals and equivocations that marked the NDP's ensuing four years in power stemmed directly or indirectly from the financial fallout and vociferous business opposi-tion aroused by that ill-fated first budget. Thereafter, the Rae gov-ernment seemed to lack the stomach or the necessary resources to take on the business community, preferring instead to trim its ideo-logical sails in the hopes of placating the ever-important foreign creditors who held a large chunk of the province's mushrooming debt. On a number of key policy initiatives, when faced with adamant business opposition, the NDP either backed away from long-standing party commitments or went into a delaying action, ensuring that no reforms would ever be implemented. This was the case with the NDP's proposed tax reforms to make the system more equitable and ensure that business paid its fair share; this proposal had been one of the most prominent promises in the *Agenda for People*. However, the Fair Tax Commission consulted broadly for almost three years before issuing its massive report, and by the time the report was released, the Rae government was both unable and unwilling to do anything about the major recommendations, which themselves re-flected deep, intractable divisions between the business community and other groups.[20]

On another key item in the *Agenda for People*, public automobile insurance, the Rae government made its most spectacular and hu-miliating retreat of all. This was the policy reversal that in all prob-ability did the most to disillusion the party's core supporters (prior to the implementation of the Social Contract, that is), since public auto insurance has long had a privileged place in social democratic mythology. While in opposition, Bob Rae had coauthored, with Mel Swart, long-time MPP from Welland-Thorold, an indictment of private automobile insurance.[21] All of that went by the wayside on the first anniversary of the NDP's election victory (September 6, 1991), when Premier Rae peremptorily announced that his government was abandoning its plans to nationalize automobile insurance. In making the announcement, Rae indicated that he accepted the arguments put forward by the insurance industry lobby that a public plan would kill thousands of jobs, saddle the government with billions of dollars in debt at a time when its coffers were virtually empty, and spawn a massive bureaucracy. Similar 180-degree turns were performed on the issues of Sunday shopping and casino gambling, both of which the NDP had condemned while it was in opposition. Once in power, confronted with an epidemic of cross-border shopping and the new economic climate of the 1990s (which meant that the desperate search for government revenues outweighed any moral opposition the NDP might have previously had to state-sponsored gambling), the Rae government quickly, and seemingly effortlessly, reversed its stance.

In all three cases — public automobile insurance, Sunday shopping, and casino gambling — the ultimate policy decision came as a surprise to many in the caucus and the party rank and file, a large proportion of whom felt that there had been little real consultation or effort to canvass opposing viewpoints. It was the manner in which these policy decisions were handed down from on high, as much as the abandonment of party ideology, that rankled grass-roots NDP supporters. These three policy reversals foreshadowed the manner in which the Social Contract would be unveiled in the spring of 1993 and reflected the hypercentralization of power around Bob Rae and a very select group of senior advisers and civil servants.

By early 1992, the NDP had embraced the language of fiscal conservatism with a vengeance. Rae and Laughren announced to their caucus that the budget deficit could not be allowed to rise above $10 billion, for fear of scaring off foreign investors, jeopardizing Ontario's credit rating, and thereby raising the cost of borrowing. In the winter of 1992–93, a number of doomsday scenarios were circulating within the senior bureaucracy: these scenarios envisaged a budget deficit that would hit $17 billion if the government did not take extreme measures to control spending. Senior officials and ministers began to fear that Ontario, like New Zealand a decade earlier, would hit the "debt wall" and be unable to borrow from foreign creditors.[22]

By this time, economic policy in Ontario was controlled by a small group of senior ministers and bureaucrats: "Rae, Laughren, deputy cabinet secretary Michael Mendelson, Treasury Board secretary Jay Kaufman, [David] Agnew [secretary of the cabinet and clerk of the Executive Council] ... deputy minister of Health Michael Decter" and, finally, Peter Warrian, who was appointed the Treasury Board's chief economist in December 1992.[23] It was within this coterie of advisers that the idea of a social contract was first hatched. On March 30, 1993, the Rae government announced its intention to roll back the wages of the employees in the broader public sector by approximately 5 per cent to realize savings of $2 billion in compensation costs.[24] The government wanted an agreement before the budget was brought down in early May 1993, allowing little more than a month to negotiate one of the most complicated deals in the province's history. In a revealing analogy, Peter Warrian described these negotiations as "a crazy process ... It's like landing a 747, where the last 500 feet is sort of a controlled crash."[25] From a political perspective, however, the "crash" was *not* controlled, leaving passengers and crew dead on the tarmac, so to speak.

How could the Ontario NDP have started down the road toward an imposed social contract — an act of electoral self-immolation, since it involved opening up signed collective agreements — possibly the most serious act of apostasy for any social democratic government to commit? In part, the answer is to be found in the technocratic hubris displayed by the leading bureaucrats and political appointees involved in the Social Contract negotiations. For instance, chief negotiator Michael Decter came to the job having just scored an impressive "victory" in the health care sector, helping to engineer a deal between the NDP and the Ontario Medical Association. He and Rae clearly believed that this magic touch would also work its wonders in the Social Contract negotiations.

The government's optimism, born of arrogance, was clearly unwarranted. After the unions[26] withdrew from the negotiations, Laughren was forced to enact Bill 48 to impose restraint on government employees. The legislation conferred enormous powers on the government and on the minister of Finance, in particular. One labour lawyer, Paul Cavalluzzo, was quoted as saying that the bill was "the most drastic intrusion into the collective-bargaining process that I've ever seen."[27]

Warrian, who succeeded Decter as chief negotiator, had consistently advised against opening the collective agreements. He contends that the decision to enact Bill 48 was "an act of political anger. It wasn't part of the plan. There was no need to do it." Once the decision to impose the Social Contract had been made, the results were depressingly predictable: a precipitous drop in NDP membership; the decline of the party (both federally and provincially) into political irrelevance and impotence, culminating in the NDP's disastrous showing in the federal election of 1993, when it won a mere nine seats (and thus lost official party status and the accompanying research monies). In addition, an ugly schism developed within the labour movement, pitting the public sector unions, along with the more militant Canadian Auto Workers (CAW), against their private sector counterparts who, after years of imposed wage cuts and lay-offs, did not sympathize with civil servants protesting the comparatively modest restraints imposed under the Social Contract.[28]

Astoundingly, some within the NDP viewed the Social Contract as a great victory, a difficult policy choice that proved the party could govern in the name of *all* Ontarians, and not just the "special interests." This was a popular theme among media pundits like Jeffrey Simpson, who were not well-known social democratic supporters, but some in the NDP caucus and rank and file shared the view. Indeed, the NDP's election advertising was in large part geared around the Social Contract, with Bob Rae proudly boasting that he would be very happy to be remembered as the premier who had imposed the restraint package. As the public opinion data in Figure 1 and the election results themselves reveal, however, the Social Contract did not halt or reverse the NDP's slide in popularity, nor, more importantly, did it enable the Rae government to make the hoped-for breakthrough into new categories of voters who had traditionally spurned the party.

It would be inaccurate and unfair to claim that the Rae government backtracked or equivocated on *every* element of its economic program. The wage protection fund (Bill 70, 1991), labour relations reform (Bill 40, 1992), the sector partnerships fund, the Ontario Training and Adjustment Board: these initiatives appealed to the NDP's core constituency in organized labour and represented significant policy innovations in the North American context. Even here, however, it is important to distinguish between government rhetoric and reality. If there is one recurrent theme interwoven through these policies, it is the NDP's desire to build on social "partnerships" to transform Ontario's economy into a high-wage, high-value-added, globally competitive system. Yet, as political scientists Jane Jenson and Paule Rianne Mahon point out, organized labour itself was bitterly divided over the desirability of this strategy, with the CAW vociferously opposed to what it saw as a class collaborationist approach.[29] Moreover, as the negotiations over the Social Contract confirmed, merely chanting the mantra of partnership is a far cry from actually achieving it. The tangible results of the sector partnerships initiatives were actually quite limited, despite the NDP government's efforts to convince the public otherwise. In the auto parts sector, for instance, one official involved in the attempt to establish a sector plan contended that the social partners simply did not wish to "dance with each other." Above all, the minister of Industry's desire for some form of agreement that could be presented to the public as concrete evidence of the utility of the sector partnerships approach drove the exercise.[30]

In summary, it can be said that some of the keystones of the Rae government's economic program, in particular the Social Contract, alienated the party's core supporters without persuading other groups of voters to endorse the NDP. By contrast, some key items in the Rae government's social program — its "equity agenda" in particular — were designed to appeal to social movement activists, who historically have had an ambivalent attitude toward the NDP. Often, these activists attacked NDP policies for being too "reformist," rather than genuinely radical. At the same time, the equity agenda confused and divided the NDP's core constituency in organized labour and antagonized large numbers of the voting public — most of whom had not previously supported the NDP.

The employment equity legislation (Bill 79), passed by the Rae government in 1993, was the target of most of the criticism and generated more controversy than almost any other NDP initiative. Not only did Bill 79 embody the Rae government's penchant for highly intrusive and bureaucratic solutions to structural or societal problems, but the manner in which the bill's advocates conducted debate over the law — by branding opponents as racists or worse — needlessly polarized and inflamed public opinion on this subject. Too often, the Rae government acted as though its good intentions obviated the need for any debate on the substance and specifics of the policy.

Much of the controversy about Bill 79 centred on the question of quotas: did the legislation enforce preferential hiring quotas for the designated minority groups (women, aboriginals, visible minorities, and persons with disabilities)? During the 1995 provincial election campaign, Mike Harris and the Conservatives very effectively drove home the message in the minds of many voters that Bill 79 was the NDP's "quota law" and that it would hobble specific categories of people — in particular, young white males — in their search for employment in these recessionary times. Strictly speaking, of course, the NDP and the law's defenders were quite right to point out that nowhere in the legislation were quotas even mentioned. Bill 79 required public sector employers with more than ten workers and private sector employers with more than fifty employees to conduct surveys of their employees to determine the proportions of the four designated groups in their workforce; prepare an employment equity plan; and "implement positive measures with respect to the recruitment, hiring, retention, treatment and promotion" of the four groups.[31] The Employment Equity Commission was established to monitor the implementation of the employment equity plans, and a tribunal was created to assess penalties for those violating the act — not a whiff of quotas in any of this.

And yet the ultimate objective of the act was to ensure that "every employer's workforce, in all occupational categories and at all levels of employment, shall reflect the representation of Aboriginal people, people with disabilities, members of racial minorities, and women in the community."[32] This provision does give one pause, for, if not by quotas, then how was this objective to be attained? Moreover, precisely how does one define "community," and how is one to measure "progress"? A consultant who worked briefly for the Employment Equity Commission (herself a member of a visible minority) has argued that the biggest drawback in the legislation was its obsession with numbers: "The numbers became a proxy for fairness."[33] In addition, the numbers themselves were tainted, since the workforce surveys allowed employees to designate themselves as members of one or another of the disadvantaged groups; moreover, employees could not be coerced into answering the surveys, though they had to return the forms, even if empty. This led to some unanticipated consequences: for example, "at one large Ontario institution in the broader public sector, more women than men chose to self-identify. Consequently, the proportion of females to males was artificially inflated, thus reducing the equity argument for hiring and promoting women."[34] One university official also noted, quite justifiably, that employers were obligated to use the self-identification results, "so if [respondents] wanted to say they were men instead of women, they could do that."[35]

Aside from the nightmarish logistical difficulties confronting the NDP's employment equity plan, there are three aspects of Bill 79 that merit further attention. First, as political scientist Reg Whitaker has forcefully argued, the law indicated that the Rae government had "swallowed the dubious notion of mirror representation ... Why should all occupational categories be mirror reflections of the exact demographic proportion of these groups in the society?"[36] Bill 79 was based on the untenable assumption that any difference between the proportion of minorities in society and that in a given occupation was *necessarily* the result of discrimination. It did not allow for the possibility that at least some of these deviations could be attributed to purely innocent differences between minorities and the majority in career choices.

Second, Bill 79 played the politics of identity and victimization in a most invidious fashion, and this certainly contributed to the powerful backlash against the law. As Whitaker again points out, the legislation penalized precisely that category of workers that had the least to do with the existing imbalance in the occupational structure: *young* white males. It was very easy for tenured white male faculty, for instance, to proclaim their enthusiasm for Bill 79, since they would not be deprived of employment because of the law. But "[y]oung, white, able-bodied males will find themselves placed at the back of employment queues and at the bottom of promotional ladders."[37] It is not difficult to see why this kind of reasoning did not sit well with organized labour,[38] especially when the employment equity commissioner herself, Juanita Westmoreland-Traore, confirmed the suspicion that sex trumped class in this brave new world. Asked by a reporter whether one of the consequences of Bill 79 might be that "the daughter of a professional couple, say a doctor and a lawyer, will have greater employment opportunities than, say, the son of an unemployed Hamilton steelworker," the commissioner responded that the son of the unemployed steelworker "still has more employment opportunities than the daughter of an upper-middle-class couple because he is not a woman. Being a woman, she says, is a basic disadvantage in the job market. That is the social and economic reality of today."[39]

Third, Bill 79 underscored the Ontario NDP's preference for heavy-handed bureaucratic responses to social problems. The new employment equity bureaucracy created by the legislation had potentially enormous powers, and thirty-two regulations outlined in the act could be rewritten at the whim of cabinet. Predictably, this struck fear in the hearts of such groups as the Canadian Federation of Independent Business and the Canadian Manufacturers Association. However, the Canadian Bar Association also issued an alarm:

> ... it is important for the government to realize that most On-
> tario workplaces do not understand what is necessary to do
> employment equity [*sic*] and, rather than providing layers and
> layers of difficult bureaucratic approach, we think it's impor-
> tant to have a simplified approach with great government sup-
> port. The critical issue of whether employment equity is
> imposed by quotas or by goals is not clear from this bill. ...
> The reason we say this is that there is the overriding authority
> of the Employment Equity Commission to substitute its own
> views for what organizations and their bargaining agents have
> concluded is appropriate. This leaves the door open for the
> imposition of quotas. The very fact that it is necessary to go to
> the regulation to find out exactly what is a goal or a timetable
> and how it will be implemented ... is sufficient proof that the
> act is incomplete.[40]

Some witnesses before the Standing Committee — including the Canadian Bar Association — questioned the need for yet another rights tribunal when the Ontario Human Rights Commission could just as easily field complaints about the implementation of employment equity.

Bill 79 was only the most notorious example of the Rae government's excessive bureaucratic zeal, its tendency to demonize opposition, and its mistaken assumption that good intentions guarantee good social policy. Certain features of the Advocacy Act and its companion legislation, as well as the long-term health care reforms, could also be cited as examples of this ultimately self-defeating mind-set. So, too, could the government's educational reforms, which culminated in the destreaming initiatives and the Common Curriculum. In each of these instances, the government tended to run roughshod over its alleged partners if the latter objected to its ultimate objectives. This was especially obvious in the education sector. Liz Barkley, then president of the Ontario Secondary School Teachers Federation, wrote of her relations with Tony Silipo, the minister of Education:

No real consultation, no apparent consultation, faulty and incomplete research, and confusion characterize the destreaming/delabelling initiatives of the Silipo ministry ... There is little teacher input to the classroom decisions of the Minister. As your official representatives, we are now having to resort to overheard messages and the outright cloak-and-dagger transmission of Ministry documents to discover what the Minister is doing. For example, our knowledge of [the policy on] the specialization years comes from a document which simply appeared on my desk, by grace of someone who felt that OSSTF might want to know what was happening. This kind of communication is not the level of consultation we expected from this government.[41]

This technocratic policy style, it is safe to say, alienated many key groups that might have been expected to support the NDP's bid for re-election. The attitude underlying the style — "we know better than you what is good for you" — would be just one of the factors contributing to the spectacular success of the so-called Common Sense Revolution.

Governing a complex province of eleven million people in an age of rapidly deteriorating economic conditions is not an easy task. It was made more difficult for Bob Rae and the NDP by the fact that a powerful and vocal business community, supported by many of the most influential organs of the popular media, impugned the very legitimacy of the government and questioned its right to govern. Add to this the tensions between the province's first social democratic government and the Queen's Park bureaucracy, and finally, stir in the conflicts within the NDP's ranks, pitting pragmatists against radicals — this would seem to be a recipe for spectacular failure.

I do not wish to minimize the obstacles confronting the NDP when it took the reins of power in 1990. And yet, its difficulties might have been eased somewhat had it paid more than just lip service to one of its favourite buzzwords — social partnership. If the NDP is ever to claw its way out of the wilderness of opposition and become relevant to the electorate once again, it will have to re-appropriate "common sense" from today's right-wing populists and begin to reimagine the nature and purpose of the public sector as well as the principal tasks of social democracy in the next millennium.[42]

The 1995 Election and the Prospects for the "Red Tory" Province

In view of the dramatic collapse in support for the Liberal party generally (and Lyn McLeod personally) during the 1995 election campaign, the Tories' victory of eighty-two seats cannot be interpreted as an unequivocal endorsement of the Common Sense Revolution (though the Tories clearly think otherwise, given the haste with which they are proceeding in dismantling any evidence of the ten years of Liberal-NDP rule). The NDP had "flatlined" in public opinion well before the election was called and was therefore not an option for the vast majority of voters, despite widespread admiration for Bob Rae's leadership qualities. In the end, then, the election was as much a referendum on Lyn McLeod's leadership and on the party's fuzzy — and pathetically derivative — Red Book as it was a ratification of the Common Sense Revolution. But there can be no denying that Harris and the Tories successfully pushed a number of "hot buttons" in the electorate, especially those concerning employment equity and workfare. Interestingly, an Insight Canada poll taken shortly after the election suggests that the Tories' message may have struck its most responsive chord among the young (voters aged 18 to 24): 46 per cent of this category claimed to have voted for the Conservatives, while 28 per cent opted for the Liberals and 15 per cent for the NDP.[43] This is precisely the category among which one would expect to find the greatest unease about the economy — and about the potential impact of employment equity on job prospects.

Almost two years into the Conservatives' mandate (as of May 1997), opinion polls suggest that a sizeable majority of Ontarians are still sympathetic to the basic thrust of the Common Sense Revolution — to reduce the size of government and eliminate waste and inefficiency. But the province is seriously polarized and many voters seem shell-shocked by the rapid pace of change. To confuse matters even further, cutbacks in the health sector, and to a lesser extent in education, are highly unpopular with many in the electorate. The revolutionaries at Queen's Park appear to have detected the flagging support among voters and backed away from some of their more grandiose visions; the privatization of Ontario Hydro and the LCBO, for instance, has apparently been abandoned, and the workfare measures have been implemented very hesitantly and unevenly. The Tories may well have engineered a noticable shift rightward in public opinion, but the early dream of some of their most militant ideologues, of duplicating the Thatcher or New Zealand experiences in Ontario, is likely to go unrealized.

Endnotes

1. Desmond Morton, "*Sic Permanet*: Ontario People and Their Politics," in Graham White, ed., *The Government and Politics of Ontario*, 4th ed., Toronto: Nelson, 1990, 6. John Wilson, in his well-known article on Ontario's "red tory" political culture, argues that the province is characterized by stability, caution, and restraint in political matters. See "The Ontario Political Culture," in Donald C. MacDonald, ed., *The Government and Politics of Ontario*, Toronto: Macmillan, 1975.
2. In 1971 the Conservatives won 45 per cent of the popular vote and 78 (66.7 per cent) of the legislature's 117 seats.
3. The author wishes to thank Marie Blythe, Laura Blythe, and Bobbi-Leigh Laurie for their research assistance on this project, which is part of a larger investigation of relations between the state, business and labour in Ontario and Quebec. The project has been funded in part by SSHRC Grant #410-94-0583.
4. These and other factors are summarized in Rand Dyck, *Provincial Politics in Canada*, 3rd ed., Toronto: Prentice-Hall, 1996, 312. See also Wilson, "Ontario Political Culture," 228. Wilson emphasizes the crucial importance of effective leadership, absence of scandal in government ranks, and the ruling party's ability "to maintain an equitable balance between the principal interests of the province..."
5. Dyck notes that the decision apparently reflected the increasing proportion of Roman Catholic residents, as well as the new intimacy between Davis and Cardinal Emmett Carter, whose frequent presence at Conservative party events had been noted. *Provincial Politics in Canada*, 347. Rosemary Speirs contends that while Davis may not have made a formal promise to Cardinal Carter to extend full funding, "Carter had come to know Davis well, to understand the naggings of his conscience, and to feel the premier would eventually set an old wrong right." *Out of the Blue*, Toronto: Macmillan, 1986, 22–6.
6. The author worked as campaign manager for the NDP candidate in Ottawa West in 1985 and can attest to the level of vitriol that marked the election. The overwhelming sentiment among voters seemed to be one of intense frustration at the refusal of all three parties to debate the issue of separate-school funding, but the Tories were the targets of most of the hostility, since it had been their former leader who had made the fateful decision. Speirs reports that Frank Miller and a number of his defeated colleagues felt that the full-funding issue had sabotaged the Tories' campaign. See *Out of the Blue*, 138–9, 146.
7. Obviously, it was not a formal coalition in which both parties were represented in the cabinet but rather an agreement be-

tween the two whereby the NDP promised to support the Liberals if certain policies were implemented.

8. See A. Brian Tanguay, "The Transformation of Canada's Party System in the 1990s," in James P. Bickerton and Alain-G. Gagnon, eds., *Canadian Politics*, Peterborough: Broadview Press, 1994, 113–40.

9. This analysis is not startlingly original, of course. Michael Bliss makes the same points forcefully in his "Foreward" in Georgette Gagnon and Dan Rath, *Not Without Cause*, Toronto: HarperCollins, 1991, xvii. Bliss writes that Peterson was among the first provincial leaders — Richard Hatfield of New Brunswick, Brian Peckford of Newfoundland, Bill Vander Zalm of B.C., and Grant Devine of Saskatchewan were the others — to be tossed onto the "ashheap" by "the same matrix of voter anger and insistence on higher standards of public performance."

10. David Peterson's wife, Shelley, was quoted as saying that "[t]his election was like 'Wack-a-Mole' ... That game they have at fairs, where the little mechanical moles stick their heads up through the holes and you hit them with a hammer. [Peterson] was the first to stick [his] head up after Meech." Gagnon and Rath, *Not Without Cause*, 392.

11. Minor parties took 6.5 per cent of the popular vote in 1990, as opposed to 2.3 per cent in 1987 and 1.3 per cent in 1985. The Family Coalition Party alone won 2.7 per cent of the vote in 1990; the Confederation of Regions Party, a virulently antibilingual organization, took more than 9 per cent of the vote in a handful of mainly northern (Algoma, Cochrane South, Nickel Belt, Sault Ste. Marie, Sudbury) and eastern (Quinte, Cornwall) ridings and 1.9 per cent provincewide. See Ontario, Chief Election Officer, *Election Returns, 1990 General Election*.

12. Thomas Walkom, *Rae Days*, Toronto: Key Porter Books, 1994, 96. The authors of the document, according to Walkom, were Chuck Rachlis and David Agnew. Gagnon and Rath contend that the *Agenda for People* was drafted only when it became obvious that Rae needed some kind of policy program to appear credible in the leaders' debate. They quote NDP strategist David Reville as saying: "We, of course, had no notion that we might ever have to implement it." *Not Without Cause*, 313–14.

13. Just prior to the 1995 election, political commentator Jeffrey Simpson made the same point: In 1990, he wrote, "Ontarians wanted the Liberals out, but they were not yet ready to bring back the Conservatives, who reminded them of the despised Mulroney government in Ottawa. The nature and structure of the victory ought to have communicated to the NDP that they were still a decidedly minority party that could win re-election only by expanding its political base; that is, by constantly demonstrating to irregular NDP voters that the party was not doctrinaire." "Ontario's NDP and the Fruit Borne from Two Poisonous Seeds," *The Globe and Mail*, June 1, 1995, A14.

14. That is, the tendency to meet with numerous groups, certain that one or two of them would likely support the policy position that had *already* been adopted.
15. The first book-length treatment of the Rae government was written by party members (on the far left) George Ehring and Wayne Roberts, and given the apposite title of *Giving Away a Miracle*, Oakville: Mosaic Press, 1993.
16. This section of the paper draws on two of my earlier articles: "On Winning the Battle and Losing the War: Labour Relations Reform in Ontario and the Crisis of Social Democracy," Paper presented to the annual meeting of the Canadian Political Science Association, Carleton University, Ottawa, June 6–8, 1993, and "Social Democracy on Trial: The Parti Québécois, the Ontario NDP, and the Search for a New Social Contract," in Jean-Pierre Beaud and Jean-Guy Prévost, eds., *La social démocratie en cette fin de siècle/Late Twentieth Century Social Democracy*, Québec: Presses de l'Univérsité du Québec, 1995, 173–200.
17. Lorne Bozinoff and Peter MacIntosh, "Ontario NDP Continues to Lose Ground," *The Gallup Report*, May 29, 1991, write that "the NDP's controversial spring budget has aroused the disdain of the Ontario public. Almost two-in-three adults (63%) aware of the document state that the budget will not serve to strengthen the provincial economy." Seventy-five per cent of those surveyed were in fact aware of the budget measures.
18. Walkom, *Rae Days*, 98–103.
19. Walkom, *Rae Days*, 103.
20. Fiona Nelson, member of the Fair Tax Commission (telephone interview), December 22, 1994.
21. *Highway Robbery*, submission to the Inquiry into Motor Vehicle Accident Compensation in Ontario (Honourable Justice Coulter A. Osborne, Commissioner), April 13, 1987.
22. Walkom, *Rae Days*, 117–20. The $17-billion figure is cited in Government of Ontario, *Jobs and Services: A Social Contract for the Ontario Public Sector, Proposals*, Queen's Printer, April 23, 1993, 3. In this document, the Ontario government notes that the International Monetary Fund "recently has warned that [Canada's] federal and provincial debt levels are unsustainable and will hamper economic recovery."
23. Walkom, *Rae Days*, 115.
24. Government of Ontario, Minister of Finance, *A Guide to the Social Contract*, Queen's Printer, July 1993, 6.
25. Peter Warrian (interview) Toronto, December 16, 1994. All of the comments attributed to Warrian are taken from this interview unless otherwise noted.
26. I do not wish to exculpate the unions entirely; clearly some of their negotiating stances were unrealistic, and their bitterness toward the NDP after the Social Contract was imposed was self-defeating. This reaction was, however, entirely understandable, and had the government not operated with such an unrealistic timetable, the rupture might have been avoided.

27. Quoted in Martin Mittelstaedt, "Dramatic Legislation Surpasses Trudeau Bill," *The Globe and Mail*, June 16, 1993, A8.
28. The historical parallels between the fate of the Parti Québécois government after its clash with public sector unions in 1982–83 and that of the Rae administration are explored in my article "Social Democracy on Trial."
29. Jane Jenson and Paule Rianne Mahon, "From 'Premier Bob' to 'Rae Days': The Impasse of the Ontario New Democrats," in Beaud and Prévost, *La social démocratie en cette fin de siècle*, 151–52, 158–62. Jenson and Mahon make the important point that the NDP did nothing, either before or after its 1990 victory, "to prepare the party and voters for the economic strategy" it intended to pursue if it took power.
30. Based on interviews with officials in the Ministry of Economic Development and Trade conducted in October and November, 1995.
31. *Statutes of Ontario* 1993, chapter 35, s. 2(4).
32. *Statutes of Ontario* 1993, chapter 35, s. 2(2).
33. Quoted in Sandra Martin, "The Inevitable Backlash," *The Toronto Star*, November 19, 1995, F4. For even more vitriolic attacks on Bill 79, see Martin Loney, "The Politics of Race and Gender," *Inroads* 3 (Summer 1994): 80–87, and Robert Martin, "Opposing Racism by Racist Means," *Inroads* 3 (Summer 1994): 88–97.
34. Martin, "The Inevitable Backlash," F4.
35. Quoted in Martin, "The Inevitable Backlash," F4.
36. Reg Whitaker, "The Cutting Edge of Ontario's Bad Law," *The Globe and Mail*, January 6, 1994, A19.
37. Whitaker, "Ontario's Bad Law," A19.
38. Walkom, *Rae Days*, 218; Jenson and Mahon, "From 'Premier Bob' to 'Rae Days,'" 164–65.
39. Andrew Dreschel, "Reversal of Fortune," *The Hamilton Spectator*, October 1, 1994, A7.
40. Legislative Assembly of Ontario, Standing Committee on Administration of Justice, September 2, 1993, J–625.
41. Liz Barkley, "Silipo's Destreaming/Delabelling Initiative: This Simplistic Approach to Social Equity May Undermine Public Education," *Education Forum — OSSTF/FEESO* (Summer 1992): 9–10. Cited in D. Marie Blythe, "Restructuring Ontario's Education System: The Role of Citizen Interest Groups in the Formation of Education Policy, 1989 to 1994," M.A. major research paper, Wilfrid Laurier University, September 1994, 60. Blythe's study is a thoughtful investigation of the gap between the Ontario NDP's rhetorical commitment to "partnership" and its actual highly technocratic and manipulative policy-making style.
42. It might profitably begin this task by reading the very interesting collection of essays by Geoff Mulgan, *Politics in an Antipolitical Age*, Cambridge MA: Polity Press, 1994.
43. Insight Canada Research, "Common Sense for Ontario: Defining the PC Mandate," Toronto, November 2, 1995. I am grateful to Charlie Angelakos of Wilfrid Laurier University for providing me with this information.

3

More than a Guard Change: Politics in the New Ontario

Peter Woolstencroft

From 1943 to 1985 the Ontario PC party formed nine majority and three minority governments. Unexpectedly, the four elections held in 1985, 1987, 1990, and 1995 produced remarkably divergent results and broke the Conservatives' seeming monopoly of power. The 1985 election heralded a minority government — not unknown in Ontario — but, for the first time, with an arrangement between the Liberals and the NDP in which, over a two-year period, the Liberals promised not to call an election and the NDP guaranteed support for the government on nonconfidence motions. Just two years later, in 1987, the Liberals swept to power, winning their first election since 1937. The 1990 election, unexpectedly called after the failure of the Meech Lake Accord, produced a most remarkable result: the NDP won a majority of seats, ushering in Ontario's first social democratic government. Then in 1995 a widely anticipated Liberal victory dissolved in the last weeks of the campaign, producing not only a strong majority for the PC party but also a government committed to a clearly right-wing platform, advertised as the Common Sense Revolution.

Highlighted by pledges to undertake a fundamental reform of the welfare system, to make significant changes in affirmative action programs and labour legislation, to slash government spending, and to cut provincial income tax by 30 per cent over three years, the Tory platform bore little resemblance to the electoral approach and style of government that had been the hallmark of the PC governments of

George Drew, Leslie Frost, John Robarts, and William Davis, from 1943 to 1985. The contrast was stark. Previous Tory governments had mastered the political art of balancing leading societal interests, prudently managing political affairs, and avoiding ideological conflict; the new style of explicit policies reflects a clear ideological design and the willingness to pit interests against each other. Instead of viewing politics in terms of an evolving consensus, the new government seems committed to systematically reversing the previous ten years of Liberal and New Democratic government.

As the Tories quickly implement central elements of their platform, most notably in the areas of welfare reform, employment equity, and government spending, Ontarians ponder the meaning of the 1995 election. Was it a normal election insofar as the winner benefitted from the public's accumulated discontent with the incumbent party and presented an alternative that attracted a winning coalition of voters, if only temporarily? Or does the Conservative victory transcend ordinary electoral dynamics and reflect a fundamental shift in political thinking within the province? That is, is it more than a guard change?

The 1995 Election

Modern elections often exhibit two salient characteristics: first, there are sudden and sharp shifts in party preferences, as measured in public opinion polls, throughout an election campaign; second, parties win in areas where they have not been serious competitors (see Chapter 6, Table 19). Electorates are volatile because traditional partisan allegiances are much weaker than they were in, say, the 1960s. Group allegiances are also considerably weaker, so individual citizens react to political events and movements with fewer attachments to intermediary social organizations. Voters, now oriented much more towards leaders and issues, are susceptible to the parties' extensive electronic advertising campaigns, which are built on sophisticated polling research. Massive changes in seats result, to the point that few constituencies fall into the "safe" category.

The two Ontario elections of 1990 and 1995 exhibited both characteristics. When the writ was dropped in 1990, the Liberals were widely believed to be invulnerable. (On the eve of the election call, Tory insiders feared that, at best, the Conservatives would win a handful of seats. Some even thought the Liberals would win all 130 seats.) But in the course of the campaign, the Liberal's issueless — some say cynical — approach imploded, and in the last two weeks the NDP catapulted out of its traditional levels of support. With just under 38 per cent of the popular vote, the NDP won a majority government, surprising all — even the NDP's most fervent partisans. The party won seats throughout the province, including constituencies where they had had only a marginal presence in the past.

In the 1995 election a substantial fraction of the Ontario electorate wanted an alternative to the highly unpopular NDP, which had doubled the provincial debt over its time in office and angered many of its traditional supporters by its revocation of public service labour contracts and abandonment of many of its campaign promises. However, once the election was called, the Liberals, favoured in the public opinion polls by over 50 per cent of the electorate for over three years, were revealed to have a number of electoral weaknesses. Not only was their support shallow (perhaps, in good measure, being merely an echo of the federal party's widespread popularity), but their leader, Lyn McLeod, was neither well known nor well regarded. And the Liberal position, precarious as it was, was undermined by the party's policies, first enunciated in a Red Book imitative of the federal Liberals' successful campaign strategy of the 1993 election, and then amended later in the campaign. Liberal policies were unfocused, seemingly addressing every worry or concern expressed by Ontarians. They were also ambiguous, designed to appear simultaneously right-wing — and therefore meant to undercut the Tories — and reformist, thus not losing voters to the New Democrats, who were warning about the dangers of voting for right-wing parties.[1]

From the standpoint of political science, the 1995 election was unusual. Generally, the distribution of political attitudes in society is such that a vast majority of people are clustered in the middle of the political spectrum. As one moves to the left and right ends, fewer and fewer adherents are found. Given this distribution, electoral success is created by putting together appeals that attract the middle range of political attitudes. "Broker" parties, primarily interested in winning office, are predicted by students of electoral politics to locate themselves in the centre of the political spectrum. Electoral positioning generally requires that parties avoid delineating their programs, delay making commitments lest the effect be nullified by opponents, and use language that unifies rather than divides.

Ontario in the postwar period exemplified the traditional electoral process. And the Liberals in 1995, for their part, played the electoral game in a way that typically had met with success. In contrast, by adopting an explicit set of policies, enunciating them well before the election was called, and clearly linking themselves with business interests, the Ontario Tories acted very much contrary to commonly held political science ideas about the behaviour of political parties.

Observers have offered a number of interpretations of the 1995 election. Hugh Segal, a long-term Tory activist and spokesperson, explains the Conservative victory as the re-emergence of the traditional three-way split in Ontario's politics, with the Tories presenting not radical but "reasonable" alternatives to the NDP. All the Tories want is to return Ontario to spending and taxation levels of 1985, the year they left office. Segal believes the Liberals failed because they ran as an incumbent party and failed to catch the desire for change.[2]

Tom Long, who served as chair of the PC campaign and is closely associated with Mike Harris, sees the election in more dramatic terms. The new premier is described as wanting to "fundamentally move the goal posts by resetting the agenda and redefining conservatism as a popular, broadbased political philosophy." Further, the election "represents a fundamental shift in the balance of power between the state on the one hand, and the private sector and the individual citizen on the other."[3]

Southam Press journalist John Ibbitson also interprets the evolution of the Ontario Conservatives from the 1980s to the 1990s in ideological terms. Right-wing "radicals," inspired by the writings of Friedrich August von Hayek (especially his antisocialist tract, *The Road to Serfdom*) and the political careers of Ronald Reagan and Margaret Thatcher, first took over PC campus organizations, and then, having made Mike Harris leader of the party and developed the Common Sense Revolution, they worked on the 1995 election campaign.[4] Some suggest that the right-wing stance taken by the Conservatives was, at heart, strategic. After the 1993 federal election, in which the national PC party suffered a devastating defeat, there was certainly much concern within Tory circles that the Reform party's success (in Ontario, one MPP elected and second-place finishes in fifty-seven of ninety-nine ridings) would spill over into the provincial arena.[5] If Reform entered the provincial election, the effect could be only to undercut the provincial PC party's support, at that time at 20 to 25 per cent, to levels that would lead to marginalization (if not elimination) of the party. The strategy of preservation, then, pulled the Tories to the right, a move that was followed by the federal Reform party's decision not to set up a provincial counterpart.[6]

Another election-based explanation stresses how the PC party prepared itself for the 1995 election.[7] Although burdened by heavy debt, by a leader who rarely received positive publicity, by third-place standing in the legislature, and by the negative spillovers from the hugely unpopular federal party, the provincial Conservatives engaged in technically sophisticated pre-election preparations.

The Tory campaign was clearly targeted to certain kinds of issues ascertained by their polling to be causes of discontent within the Ontario electorate, particularly the middle and skilled working classes. A year before the election was called, the party issued its Common Sense Revolution, which delineated the Tories' thinking on three themes: reduction of government spending (and a concomitant tax cut), welfare reform, and employment equity. Further, not only had the PC party identified, through its polling research, the issue points on which the Ontario electorate felt the NDP government had seriously mismanaged things, it also had a clear idea about what the course of the election campaign would be. That is, it predicted that the initial weeks of the campaign would show little movement of voters between the parties; the onset of advertising would mark the commencement of movements in voters' preferences, and the Liberals would fall because of their inability or unwillingness to address the critical issues on the minds of many voters. The NDP, for its part, would have only one card to play — the perception that Bob Rae was an outstandingly competent and intelligent leader — but it would have no capability to stop the Tory surge.

The role of the party in the preparation of the PCs' election manifesto has been subject to varied interpretations. One version has it that the Common Sense Revolution reflected a long period of heightened involvement by party members in the years between the 1990 and 1995 elections.[8] Another is that the clear ideological thrust and details of the party's program were the handiwork of a few close associates of Mike Harris.[9]

There is another angle to the story. The notion of the Tories being on top of their electoral positioning is belied by how the party handled the issue of photo radar. The Conservatives opposed photo radar and promised that they would eliminate it if elected. In an interview, a Tory insider suggested that the party's thinking was driven primarily by frustration about the media's lack of attention to the PCs' pre-election preparations. Needing something to call attention to itself, tacticians hit upon the idea of announcing the party's opposition to photo radar at a photo radar location.[10]

Changes in Ontario's Political Culture

But there were changes within the Conservative party that suggest the 1995 election was more than a tactical phenomenon or a function of sophisticated pre-election preparations.[11] Since the election of 1987, the political thinking in the party has undergone two shifts that reflect changes in the wider society. The first shift was reflected in the adoption of the "one person, one vote" method of leadership selection. Responding to increasing populism in Canadian political culture and heightened disquietude with élite-dominated political processes, in 1990 the party dropped the leadership convention (a tradition dating from the early 1920s) in favour of individual party members' choosing the party's leader in a format akin to a general election. The Ontario Tories, in having the first "one member, one vote" leadership election in English-speaking Canada, set the stage for its rapid adoption by other parties, both provincial and federal.[12]

The second change was reflected in the language of political discourse evident in the party's discussions, especially in terms of policy issues. Political language in the party prior to the 1990 election reflected the balancing of philosophical orientations and interests that political scientist John Wilson has identified as being the heartbeat of Ontario politics.[13] Generally it seemed that the PC party comprised three political orientations, each representing about a third of party activists. One was in the "progressive" tradition that was prepared to employ — sometimes happily, sometimes begrudgingly — the use of the state to achieve social and economic goals. Another third, in the "conservative" camp, resented what they saw as the ever-widening influence of the state and rising taxes and called for the party to move toward a more market-oriented and fiscally conservative approach. The final third saw itself as a bridge between the "progressive" and "conservative" wings of the party. Internal party elections and leadership conventions were often divided along the "progressive" and "conservative" lines, with the result determined by how the middle third of the party voted. Candidates ran for office with their appeal built on statements designed to win support from the two extreme camps and, indeed, to attract support from the middle group because of its ability to bridge the "progressives" and the "conservatives." For example, candidates talked about how they would ensure that the safety net and fundamental social policies would be maintained and protected within the context of sound fiscal management;

to the Tories, it was clear that the Liberals and others were not seriously committed to doing this!

In the two leadership conventions of 1985, each wing of the party was able to claim one of its own as party leader. Frank Miller, who became leader in the first 1985 convention and who was clearly on the right of the political spectrum, led the party to unexpected defeat in the election of that year. Larry Grossman, the leading representative of the party's "progressive" forces, won the leadership in the second 1985 convention. Under his leadership the party was shellacked in the 1987 election; one effect of Grossman's defeat was that "progressive" forces migrated to the provincial Liberals, leaving the party in the hands of more conservatively minded members. The 1990 leadership election produced few differences between the two candidates, but the eventual winner, Mike Harris, soon signalled a rightward shift in the party. In the 1990 election that followed a few months after his victory, he single-mindedly portrayed himself as "the taxfighter."[14]

Since 1990, the language of the party — both internally and externally — has changed remarkably, with the word *progressive* disappearing to a great extent. It has been supplanted by fiscally conservative, market-oriented talk. The new language of Ontario conservatism has little to say about the positive role of the state: now the state is the problem, to be reduced as much as possible so that the market can operate without constraint. A party for which observers once used language such as "red tory" to account for its electoral success and approach, now affirmed individualism and voluntarism, eschewed the evolution of the modern state structure, championed privatization, even of long-standing institutions such as Ontario Hydro, and spoke enthusiastically about the need to position Ontario to compete successfully in the international market place.

Why this change in the party?

Of course, there is no simple answer to such a general question. Three factors, however, appear to be central to the understanding of the increasing individualism evident in Ontario's politics. American conservatism, particularly in its strong market orientation and antistatism, has had a strong effect on Canadian politics, with Ontario Conservatives not being exempt. Consider the opening sentence of the Common Sense Revolution: "Government isn't working anymore. The system is broken." Conservatively oriented business and political commentators such as David Frum, Andrew Coyne, Terence Corcoran, and Ted Byfield approach political issues using the language of individualism and market-based economics and opposing the political styles of post–World War II Canada.

For its part, the Reform party, in its fixation on the deficit issue and the need to produce balanced budgets, shares many policy positions with the Republican party in the United States.[15] More deeply, the philosophical commitments of the Reform party — equality of individuals and equality of provinces — are intimately connected with central presuppositions of American political culture. The Reform party's advocacy of a "Triple E" Senate and its opposition to constitutional reform proposals not based on equal constitutional standing for all provinces introduces into Canadian constitutional discourse concepts inspired by the operation of the American Senate and the workings of the American federal system.

Specific links between the Ontario Conservatives and the Republican party are largely unexplored. Two journalistic accounts indicate that there has been some cross-border sharing of personnel. David Frum, in an article in an Air Canada publication celebrating the close ties between Canada and the United States, writes about the influence of Frank Luntz. An American who had worked with the Reform party in 1993 and on the construction of Newt Gingrich's Contract with America, the Republican party's manifesto for the 1994 congressional elections, Luntz was involved in the development of the Common Sense Revolution.[16] Mike Murphy, another American with strong links to the Republican party, has been described as having had pre-election discussions with the Conservatives about electoral strategy and their policy approach.[17]

The Charter of Rights and Freedoms, a part of Canada's political system for almost fifteen years, has also fostered a preoccupation with individual rights. Although the charter itself melds some elements of collective rights with its listing of individual rights, the overall effect of discussion about rights is to reinforce individualism. People think of themselves as individuals possessing rights and interpret this idea as meaning that the state should be limited in its ability to interfere with their behaviour. And policies that differentiate between individuals are seen as violating the rights of citizens.

Another individualizing effect is found in the development of the welfare state itself. With its various education, health, welfare, and income security programs designed to provide equality of opportunity and some measure of equality of condition, the welfare state has been presumed to lead inexorably to greater egalitarianism and collectivism. However, in his examination of the defeat in the 1990s of the social democrats in Sweden, often taken to be the exemplar of the welfare state, Swedish political scientist Bo Rothstein argues that the successful development of the welfare state may have contrary effects. People, liberated (as it were) by the security of the welfare state and provided with various capacities in their workplaces, commercial relationships, and tenancies, become dissatisfied with state-based and state-monopolized programs and demand choice, efficiency, and private providers.[18] Rothstein argues, then, that at some point in its evolution the welfare state creates attitudes partial to choice and competition. Such a development is problematic for the left because it believes that appropriate actions for resolving social problems and addressing inequalities are to be found in terms of state-centred policies and programs rather than nonstate providers; standardization and universal entitlements are valued over choice and efficiency, the very characteristics that are highly valued in the new political culture.

The individualization of Ontario's political culture can be seen in the strong negative reactions to the NDP's affirmative action programs and expansion of welfare and other social programs. It can also be seen in the increasing interest in nonstate providers of education, health, and day care. The NDP government that took office in 1990 assumed that its election reflected an electorate that had moved to the left. But a contrary interpretation is that, for many people who voted NDP in 1990, the decision was tactical, arising out of their disaffection with the Liberals and the Tories, and not ideological in character. Ironically, as the province witnessed its first social democratic government, the political culture of Ontario was undergoing a pivotal change towards individualism.

While Ontario's political culture has been influenced by internal forces, the impact of external developments has been considerable and perhaps even more significant, particularly within business circles.

Two External Forces

An important shift in political thinking has occurred in Ontario. But what happens in the province is more a function of external forces than internal ones. It is probable that there would have been severe cuts in provincial spending, although fewer and smaller cuts than the Tories have made, no matter who won the 1995 election. (The NDP and the Liberals did not commit themselves to income tax cuts.) The details undoubtedly would differ, but a Liberal or an NDP government would have moved in the direction undertaken by the Conservatives. For instance, although it was not introduced in the legislature, the NDP government did consider legislation similar to that initiated by the Conservative government regarding drug expenses for senior citizens.

The federal Liberals, in making deficit reduction a priority and reducing conditional transfers to the provinces, have commenced to reform fundamental components of the Canadian welfare state. The New Democratic governments in Saskatchewan and British Columbia are undertaking reform of their welfare systems in ways similar to those anticipated in Ontario. And in Quebec Lucien Bouchard's Parti Québécois government has moved to bring that province's huge budgetary deficits under control by proposing massive cuts in public expenditures.

The underlying facts facing the Harris government were the accumulated debt of almost $100 billion and the annual deficit of about $10 billion. Ontario's fiscal situation was the worst per capita of any province in Canada, with the possible exception of Quebec. Any party, whether in government or opposition, would have had to confront those figures in developing its fiscal strategies. And unlike Alberta — with which it is often compared — Ontario could not expect a resource boom to produce a windfall for the provincial treasury.

The expansion of the provincial state in Ontario, with its concomitant increases in taxes and borrowing in the last decade, occurred as Ontario's economic development became increasingly subject to globalization and international trade competition. Two different effects flow from this convergence.

First, differences in taxation and other input charges (such as licencing fees and regulatory requirements) are becoming increasingly important to those who decide where economic investment will occur. Ontario, benefiting from its enormous resource wealth, location on the Great Lakes system, and federal-provincial policies directed toward the development of an industrial economy, now confronts economic decision-making in which natural resources count for less, location is of diminished importance, and free trade agreements have removed the possibility of state-based economic policies. The increasing autonomy of capital has been matched by the development of technologically based industries that are not tied to particular geographic locations, and "spaceless" economic activities mean that governments must establish environments congenial to business investment and economic growth. A critical factor in fostering conditions that lead to investment is control of levels and changes in taxation.

The Canada-U.S. Free Trade Agreement and the North America Free Trade Agreement have led to borderless economies in North America. The integration of the North American economy — cogently illustrated in March 1996 by the rapid spread of layoffs at General Motors factories in Canada, the United States, and Mexico as the direct result of strikes at plants in Ohio — means that the policy options for the Ontario provincial government are constrained: it is no longer possible to think in terms of an Ontario steel or automobile industry. Globalization of economic processes means that it makes little sense to talk about independent provincial (or, for that matter, national) economic systems. Globalization of economies means that the policy bias will be against intervention in economic decision-making and adverse to redistributive policies.

The second effect refers to the financing of public policies. Since the middle 1980s Ontario's public debt has ballooned, with debt payments now constituting the third-largest item in the provincial budget, behind health and education. The fiscal crisis of the provincial state is such that no party can afford to exacerbate the province's precarious situation by increasing borrowing. In fact the pressure to cut spending programs is so strong because of the accumulating effects of budgetary deficits that any party in office would be compelled to make massive cuts, and this pressure is heightened by the federal government's dramatic reductions in transfers to the provinces.

The policy imperative for provinces will be to provide an environment in which business enterprises will be able to compete for both external and internal markets. The bias in policy-making will be to reduce the province's exposure to rapid shifts in economic conditions, particularly changes in interest rates; this bias will lead to the reduction, even elimination, of expensive spending programs — especially those based on the principle of universal entitlements.

The last five years in Ontario exemplify the weaknesses of the provincial state. The working premise of the NDP government in its first two years of office was that it was possible to have a "made-in-Ontario" policy. By maintaining and expanding programs that were paid for with borrowed money, the NDP presumed that it would be possible to alleviate, if not reverse, the worsening unemployment arising from the severe recession that hit North America. However,

the effect of government spending on economic growth and employment was marginal, even in the short term, and significantly increased the province's debt, in the long term. The 1993 Social
Contract initiative of the NDP government was a classic example of
"too little, too late," as the government belatedly recognized that its
first two years in office had exacerbated the province's economic
situation. By reversing the direction of public policy, the NDP antagonized its traditional supporters without gaining much beyond
applause from business. In effect, it adopted new language. In its first
years in office, the NDP consciously downplayed the word *competitive*, speaking instead in terms of *productivity*; in its latter years,
competitive became the watchword as the NDP — and social democratic parties around the world — grappled with the realization that
the state could not be the engine of economic growth and that the
policy imperative was to establish an environment congenial to business investment.

Political Culture and Political Processes

Much has been made about the character of political culture in
Canada. One important interpretation describes the pattern of attitudes, beliefs, and opinions in terms of regionalism, with the province of residence being, after language, the most important predictor
of differences amongst Canadians.[19] For its part, Ontario has been
described as having a distinct political culture with important elements being a combination of caution and reformism expressed in
the idea of "progressive conservatism."[20] Its party system has traditionally been marked by three competitive political parties reflecting
the diversity of the province's political culture. Eventually, some
observers have predicted, industrialization and urbanization will lead
to political interests coalescing around the polarities of the class
structure, culminating in the elimination of one party and the establishment of a two-party system, with one party oriented toward the
interests of the working class and the other championing business
interests.[21] An alternate model suggests that globalization of economies means that locally based political debates and processes prem-
ised on the ability of the provincial state to be interventionist and
redistributive will be increasingly marginalized. Changes in the
structure of Ontario's political economy will lead to the restructuring
of major political processes and the attenuation of distinctiveness in
Ontario's political culture — because what is happening in Ontario
will be similar to what will happen in the other provinces.

In general, the political processes of Ontario have contained strong elements of corporatism and pluralism. Political parties, both during and between elections, have worked closely with interest groups — the intermediaries between the state and the individual citizen — to incorporate major societal interests into the design of public policies, and in so doing have moderated social conflict and integrated major groups. In the era of the limited state and increasing individualism, parties will avoid being caught in the interest group arena as they seek to build successful electoral coalitions by appealing to individual citizens and jostling over the issue of which party has the key to economic growth.[22] Notice how the Tories since 1995 have distanced themselves from the legal profession, the Ontario Medical Association, and various teacher organizations. Parties of the centre and the right will have an advantage because of the aforementioned policy imperatives. But what of the left?

The globalization of economies raises fundamental questions about the future of social democracy as a political philosophy. The core of traditional social democratic thought has been the assertion that the state will be the mechanism for the resolution of conflict between the working and non-working classes. The state becomes the vehicle for determining the nature of economic relationships and the direction of economic growth. The commitment to equality on the part of social democrats leads to support for redistributive policies that have the effect of either moving wealth from the top ranks of society to the bottom or providing access to public goods such as health or education regardless of people's economic circumstances. Attenuation of state power means that social democracy has had to reexamine its fundamental postulate that the state will be the primary agent for social and economic change. Indeed, the NDP in Ontario, at least as represented by Bob Rae, seemed to have eventually accepted the argument that the state's role in the future would be qualitatively different than the party had imagined in the period since World War II.

Future of Politics in Ontario

What will be the consequences of this change in the role of the state for the future of politics in Ontario?

Globalization will not reduce class differences. Indeed, it may deepen them, leading to intensification of class conflict. But the traditional arena for the resolution of class-based issues — the state through public policies — will not be as significant as it was in the past. All parties, whatever their positions on the traditional political spectrum, will have to operate within the policy imperatives and biases arising from the globalization of economics.

The constrained state will pose important questions about the character of political competition — the lifeblood of liberal democracy — as parties deal with the new role of the state. Political theorist C.B. Macpherson, at the end of *Democracy in Alberta*, contemplates the future of parties in capitalist liberal democracies under the conditions of quasicolonialism and independent commodity production.[23] Looking at Alberta — and then more widely at the case of Canada in relation to the United States — he predicts the formation of a "quasi-party" system in which parties as ordinarily understood operate without the competitive representation of interests normally found in the capitalist liberal democracies. Instead, the party system is characterized by one dominant party, on the one hand, with ineffective and insignificant opposition parties, on the other. The dominant party, employing the language of "good" government, reflects the interests of the capitalist class. Its dominance, however, is contingent, for when it no longer reflects the needs of the capitalist class, it will be quickly replaced.

The conditions in provinces such as Ontario are different from those postulated by Macpherson. But the "quasi-party" system he predicted may well take hold as parties and electorates operate in a political system transformed by changes in the nature of electoral politics and the nature of the state. Sudden swings in preferences, massive changes in seats, and political debate limited by the character of the constrained state will be the characteristics of the new party system.

The Tory victory in Ontario reflected the convergence of two factors. First, the party employed a very sophisticated polling system to ascertain the "hot buttons" in the Ontario electorate. Its well-focused advertising campaign resulted in both a sudden shift in preferences in the latter stages of the campaign and the winning of a considerable number of constituencies where the party, even in its recent glory days, had not been a strong contender. Second, the overextension of the state, in light of global economic trends, resulted in a strong reaction on the part of the Ontario electorate to what seemed to be both increasing debt and ever-increasing taxes without appreciable improvement in the quality of life and in economic prospects.

The nature of political debate in Ontario will be fundamentally changed as the province confronts the globalization of its economy. The Conservatives, Liberals and New Democrats will try to stake out viable electoral territory in which the bounds of practical debate will be narrowly defined compared to what they knew even in the 1980s. The centre of Ontario's political culture will move to the right. However, even in the electronic age, political culture does not change overnight! Thus, Ontario will probably experience some softening of the rightward shift seen in 1995. Perhaps it will become evident when the Tories attempt to ameliorate the harshness of the politics of deficit reduction by committing themselves to some expansion of government spending. If the Harris Tories put the province's finances on the track to balanced budgets and retirement of debt and can provide the climate to generate 725,000 jobs over five years, they will be strong contenders to win the next election. If not the Tories, the Liberals or the New Democrats will be guards in waiting.

The party that wins the next election is much less consequential than the issue of the character of politics in Ontario. Economics, say economists, is international, pointing in the direction of stateless exchanges and relationships. All politics, say political scientists, is local. What will be the intersection between the internationalizing effects of economics and the localizing effects of politics? The prediction of a "quasi-party" system for Ontario leaves unanswered the issue of how Ontarians' interests will be served by the limited state and its constrained political processes.

Endnotes

1. See Christina Blizzard, *Right Turn: How the Tories Took Ontario*, Toronto: Dundurn Press, 1995.
2. Hugh D. Segal, "Ontario: A New Conservative Beachhead?," paper presented to The Canadian Seminar, Harvard University Centre for International Affairs, February 12, 1996.
3. Tom Long, "What the Conservative Win in Ontario Means for All of Canada," *Fraser Forum* (November 1995): 5–14.
4. John Ibbitson, "The New Blue Machine," *The Ottawa Citizen*, February 3, 1996, B1.
5. For a discussion of the federal election from the standpoint of the federal party, see Peter Woolstencroft, "'Doing Politics Differently': The Conservative Party and the Campaign of 1993," in Alan Frizzell, Jon H. Pammett, and Anthony Westell, eds., *The Canadian General Election of 1993*, Ottawa: Carleton University Press, 1994, 9–26.
6. See Blizzard, *Right Turn*, 64–6.
7. Blizzard, *Right Turn*.

8. Comments by Peter Van Loan, president of the Ontario Progressive Conservative Association, "The Ontario Election," panel organized by the Public Affairs Association of Canada, Toronto, October 11, 1996.
9. Christina Blizzard writes that "rumour has it that the idea for the Common Sense Revolution was hatched in the winter of 1993-1994 over bottles of wine and bowls of mussels at a small restaurant called Episode, a few blocks from Maple Leaf Gardens." *Right Turn*, 54.
10. Confidential interview, August 1995.
11. Although the following discussion speaks in general terms, the regional diversity is here acknowledged. There is a voluminous literature about Ontario's political culture, which is discussed comprehensively in Rand Dyck, *Provincial Politics in Canada*, 3rd ed., Scarborough: Prentice-Hall Canada Inc., 1996.
12. See Peter Woolstencroft, "'Tories Kick Machine to Bits': Leadership Selection and the Ontario Progressive Conservative Party," in Ken Carty, Lynda Erickson, and Don Blake, eds., *Leaders and Parties in Canadian Politics: Experiences of the Provinces*, Toronto: HBJ-Holt, 1992, 203–25.
13. John Wilson, "The Red Tory Province: Reflections on the Character of the Ontario Political Culture," in Donald C. MacDonald, ed., *The Government and Politics of Ontario*, 2nd ed., Toronto: Van Nostrand Reinhold, 1980, 221–23.
14. Mike Harris in his first speeches in the legislature after the 1990 election used language that presaged the approach taken by the Conservatives in the 1995 election; the focus and theme of his speeches dealt with the province's worsening debt situation and its effect on the economy.
15. The Reform and Republican parties are less united on social policy issues, reflecting, perhaps, the much weaker social base of Christian-based political action in Canada.
16. David Frum, "We are alike, eh?," *enRoute*, Montreal, Air Canada, October 1995. 17. Frum, at the close of his article, writes that Canadians are participants in a common North American culture and that those shared values "provide a glimpse of what the future may hold for the entire world — if we're lucky."
17. See the series, "The New Jersey Connection," *The Toronto Star*, February 18,19, and 20, 1996.
18. Bo Rothstein, "The Crisis of the Swedish Social Democrats and the Future of the Universal Welfare State," *Governance*, Vol. 6, No. 4 (October 1993): 492–517, especially pages 505–10.
19. Richard Simeon and David Elkins, "Provincial Political Cultures in Canada," in Elkins and Simeon, *Small Worlds*, Toronto: Methuen, 1980.
20. John Wilson, "The Red Tory Province."
21. See, e.g., John Wilson and David Hoffman, "Ontario, a Three-Party System in Transition," in Martin Robin, ed., *Canadian Provincial Politics*, Scarborough: Prentice-Hall, 1971.

22. The language of politics in recent years has contained sharp condemnation of "special interests," a term that encompasses a wide range of social and economic claimants but not business-oriented groups.

23. C.B. Macpherson, *Democracy in Alberta: Social Credit and the Party System*, Toronto: University of Toronto Press, 1953. For an extended critique, see E.A. Bell, *Social Classes and Social Credit in Alberta*, Montreal: McGill-Queen's University Press, 1993.

4

The Ontario Political Culture at the End of the Century

John Wilson

It is rapidly becoming customary to insist that the character of Ontario's political life is in the midst of a profound change. The traditional values that have been said to dominate the politics of the province almost since its inception are being rejected — if they have not already been dismissed — in the face of the inescapable advance of modern technology and the anger of an electorate too long ignored by government and newly terrified by the possibility of economic insecurity.

There has been a massive swing to the right in the province, Ontarians are told, as the end of the twentieth century approaches. The sentiments that encouraged the quite extraordinary strength of the Reform party in the 1993 and 1997 Canadian federal elections — and that are also believed to be prevalent in the United States — represent, it is said, a new way of understanding the nature of the political process and the proper role of government. The traditional Ontario political culture, in a word, is a thing of the past.

On the face of things, it is difficult to fault this analysis. It is abundantly clear that the new PC government at Queen's Park is quite unlike its NDP and Liberal predecessors in almost every respect. It also appears to have very little connection with the customary attitudes of the PC party in Ontario, and yet it managed in 1995 to attract just as solid a level of voter support as had been common during the period of continuous Conservative rule, from 1943 to 1985.

But particular governments — and especially relatively untried ones — have little to do with the political culture of any community. They are collections of people who may be in power only briefly, and if that is so, it makes no more sense to view the arrival of the Harris Conservatives in office as heralding a major political cultural change in Ontario than it did to make the same interpretation of the 1990 victory of the Rae New Democrats.

As a concept, political culture never simply describes the policies of governments. Instead, it provides a means of understanding, in the broadest sense, the political attitudes of the people of a particular society.[1] No doubt it is possible to infer some relationship between the two by recognizing that the people have chosen a specific government together with its policies, but to move from that quite crude connection to the claims that are now being made for the state of things in Ontario is unjustified.

Of course, political cultures can and do change, but they don't change overnight. The very nature of the concept — which refers to the root values and capacities of a political society — obviously suggests that change at that level will come only gradually and perhaps even imperceptibly. In short, drawing the grand conclusion that Ontario has entered a new age is surely premature without some careful reflection on the facts of the case.

The Origin of the Ontario Political Culture

Nonetheless, one central characteristic of Ontario politics does seem to have changed. Stability in government can no longer, apparently, be taken as a given in the province. After a third of a century of unbroken Liberal rule, from 1871 to 1905, and eighty years of barely interrupted Conservative domination, Ontario has had three changes of government in the last ten years.

But stability alone was never really the hallmark of the Ontario political culture. It was simply a fact of the province's political existence, created by the ability of an Oliver Mowat — or of different Conservative premiers — to reflect in their governments the essential will of the people. They did, in short, what was expected of them, and they were rewarded because they were in touch with the leading values of Ontario politics.

There is now a considerable literature outlining the origin and character of the principal elements of those values. At their root lies the idea of what S.J.R. Noel has called "managerial efficiency." In the beginning, the most obvious example of this idea was the behaviour of the military. An efficient administration was therefore thought to resemble "a well-run regiment; its officers were expected to be authoritarian yet at the same time paternalistic in their concern for the welfare of all ranks." As the nineteenth century developed, the appearance of a prosperous agrarian society provided a new model for the original conception. An efficient administration now came to be seen as "one that resembled a well-run farm; it was expected to be economical but also progressive in outlook and con-cerned with the betterment of the whole estate." In short, the idea of husbandry — in its broadest sense — became the most important value of the Ontario political culture.[2]

These ideas were easily married with the important role of the state in Ontario society.[3] They translated naturally in the twentieth century into a demand for government that administered the province not only with efficiency and care for all its citizens, but with an eye to conservation and preservation in such things as the management of Ontario's vast forest, mineral, and hydroelectric resources. Good government came to mean not simply good leadership — as is so often said of modern Ontario — but careful leadership. This defini-tion goes beyond merely a capacity for showing people where to go and what to do. It is leadership that is, almost by definition, cautious (as Mowat taught us) but that also includes both the ideas of mana-gerial efficiency and a capacity to maintain a balance among the principal interests of the province — which may be simply a descrip-tion for a more democratic age of the paternalism that flourished in Upper Canada in the nineteenth century.

This way of describing the character of the Ontario political cul-ture in the twentieth century originated in a careful analysis of the circumstances surrounding the five occasions between 1867 and 1971 (ignoring 1871 as being more technical than real), when incum-bent governments had been defeated: 1905, 1919, 1923, 1934, and 1943. The argument was that, on these occasions, a statement was being made about what was acceptable political practice in Ontario, and because those occasions were so rare, they had to be regarded as notable.[4]

In each case a government was being dismissed, presumably be-cause it did not measure up to the level of performance expected by the Ontario people. But what made these events so striking was the fact that on each occasion unusually large numbers of people — often as much as a quarter of the electorate — changed their vote, suggest-ing that what was being observed went beyond simple dissatisfaction to an expression of general political values. I set out to discover the issues on each of these occasions and the particular capacities that the leading players possessed.

The results of this research support the ideas about Ontario's political culture that I describe earlier. At every defeat the competence of the incumbent government's leadership was very much in question — not just in terms of efficiency, but also in terms of common sense. But there was more to it than that. On each occasion there was also loose in the province a feeling that the government had somehow lost touch with the people, had become, perhaps, arrogant in office, and was no longer able or willing to balance fairly the different interests of Ontario society. There was, in other words, a kind of collectivism being expressed that made demands on behalf of all sectors of the provincial community.

It was from this detailed analysis that the principal elements for political success in Ontario were drawn. It was said, in short, that in removing an administration, the people of Ontario were rejecting a particular set of attitudes and capacities for government and were thereby making a statement about fundamental political values. A more thorough analysis would also have examined the characteristics of the leadership groups who were rejected when an incumbent government was returned to office, on the assumption that their rejection would similarly offer a measurement of the demands made by the Ontario electorate. There seems little doubt that such an exercise would reveal the same conclusion: that the people of Ontario place a high value on the capacity to manage the province's affairs competently and on the ability to balance fairly the differing claims of the principal interests in the province.

The one side of this dominant pattern of values stressing the necessity of competent leadership and efficient management is very conservative. The other, focusing on fair play for everyone, is clearly progressive. The inevitable conclusion was that Ontario was best described as a "red tory" province, quite different from any other part of Canada. From the perspective of the 1970s, it seemed certain to at least one observer that any government capable of passing the twin tests for acceptable leadership could "go on at Queen's Park for ever."[5]

The End of the Conservative Dynasty

There are many reasons for supposing that this kind of analysis of the period from the 1970s on will prove useful in trying to understand

Table 2
Party Support or Abstention in Ontario Elections Since 1971

Year	Abstentions %	change	Conservatives %	change	Liberals %	change	NDP %	change	Others %	change	Net Change
1971	27		33		20		20		*		
		+6		-9		+3		-1		+1	10
1975	33		24		23		19		1		
		+2		+2		-2		-1		-1	4
1977	35		26		21		18		*		
		+7		none		-2		-6		+1	8
1981	42		26		19		12		1		
		-3		-3		+4		+2		none	6
1985	39		23		23		14		1		
		-1		-8		+7		+2		none	9
1987	38		15		30		16		1		
		-2		none		-9		+8		+3	11
1990	36		15		21		24		4		
		+2		+13		-2		-11		-2	15
1995	38		28		19		13		2		

The figures shown are the percentage share of each party's vote of the total registered electorate (rather than of total valid votes cast), with the first column representing the percentage who abstained. For each election the change in each of these percentage shares from the previous election is also shown, and in the last column the total of these changes (ignoring signs) divided by two indicates the actual number of people (as a percentage of the total registered electorate) who changed their vote. This figure must also, in the nature of the case, include people who had newly joined the electorate or left it since the last election. Figures cast in the same way for earlier Ontario elections may be found in my chapter "The Ontario Political Culture," in Donald C. MacDonald, ed., *Government and Politics of Ontario*, 1st ed., Toronto: Macmillan, 1975, 218-219. The source for both sets of figures is the *Return from the Records* for each election, compiled by the Chief Election Officer for Ontario.
* Less than half of one percent

changes since the end of the Robarts era and in making sense of the condition of the Ontario political system at the end of the twentieth century.

It has seemed to me for some time that political scientists habitually look at modern Ontario politics in the wrong way. We start with the image that our history will not allow us to ignore: the unbroken forty-two years of Conservative rule, from 1943 to 1985, with its emphasis on cautious reform in the Mowat tradition. We end with the comparative chaos that has followed since 1985: three different parties in power, all in the space of ten years. But that observation is far too simple. If we look instead at the period since the election of 1971 in the way I looked at earlier elections, we find a strikingly different picture of the significance of government defeats. Table 2 shows support for the parties in each provincial election from and including 1971 in terms of percentage shares of the registered electorate and thereby illustrates the varying strength of abstentions (which intuitively must be important when we consider the relatively low levels of turnout in recent Ontario elections).

Public recollection of the Davis years is confusing. There is a sense of general satisfaction with the premier's conduct of affairs, more or less right down to the end. But a close examination of the data presented in Table 2 shows that, far from being a continuation of the comfortable rule of his predecessors, Davis's time as premier was in reality a period of profound uncertainty. After what may now be viewed as the "honeymoon" election of 1971 — only short months after Davis had narrowly won the party leadership[6] — his government was reduced to minority status in 1975 and then kept there in 1977. Careful study of the 1981 Conservative victory will also show that it was far from being the restoration of the status quo it was thought to be at the time. And then in 1985, everything fell apart for the Conservative dynasty.

Indeed, the whole period since 1971, with few exceptions, looks and feels more like a time of continuous confrontation with government than the comparative peace to which Ontarians had supposedly become accustomed. But if that is the case, then, following the lines of the earlier analysis, there are questions to be asked that have generally been ignored in the intervening years. To begin, it seems abundantly clear that for present purposes the election of 1975 ought to be regarded as a Tory defeat. The Conservatives lost nearly ten percentage points from 1971 in the registered electorate (as shown in Table 2) or, in comparative terms, almost as much as the NDP lost between 1990 and 1995. They were no better off in terms of seats than they were ten years later when the Liberals replaced them with the help of the NDP,[7] and it is very likely that the only reason change did not take place in 1975 was that the NDP, by an accident of support distribution, was then the largest opposition party.[8] Two years later nothing had changed (except that the Liberals had again become the leading opposition party), so that while the 1977 election cannot strictly be called a government defeat, it is clearly an extension of what can be viewed as a continuing rejection of the Conservative party or, perhaps, of the leadership style of the Davis government.

At the beginning of his tenure as premier, Bill Davis exhibited a kind of truculent arrogance, acting as if he had inherited by right the leadership of Ontario. This attitude did not sit well in comparison to the stamp John Robarts had left upon the office. By the end Davis had become the quintessential procrastinator, increasingly unable, apparently, to make a firm decision — again in stark contrast to his predecessor. Clare Westcott, his executive assistant, began to complain that while caution in government was a hallmark of the Ontario tradition, it was not supposed to be carried to the point of paralysis. At a farewell roast, Westcott told of once asking Davis if he had trouble making up his mind. Davis answered, "Well, yes and no."[9]

Both extremes called into question the quality of Davis's leadership. The government was nearly brought down in 1975 by this arrogance — manifested, for example, in Davis's absolute support of a controversial federal proposal to build an airport in Pickering and the careless and inconsiderate way in which regional government was imposed on a number of less than enthusiastic municipalities, along with a series of minor scandals over the granting of contracts (scandals that Ontarians have become used to). Indeed, it is not too much to say that the NDP's new role as official opposition came about because of the seats won in areas that were affected by the Pickering proposal and that were not ordinarily NDP ridings.

The lesson was not immediately learned. As if the Ontario people had merely got their numbers wrong in 1975, Davis contrived to have his MPPs defeated in the legislature over a comparatively minor matter early in 1977 and then insisted that they were bound by constitutional practice to resign.[10] Again, the electorate, clearly annoyed by the cavalier way in which democratic government was being conducted in Ontario, refused to produce a majority, although there was a fractional increase in the Conservative vote.

As mentioned above, in analyzing the significance of leadership in Ontario politics, we should consider the capacities not just of those in power but also of the opposition party leaders. If defeats are occasions on which the people of the province are expressing their

Table 3	
Ontario Party Leaders Since 1935	
Conservatives	
Until 1938	Earl Rowe
1938-48	George Drew
1948-49	T.L. Kennedy
1949-61	Leslie Frost
1961-71	John P. Robarts
1971-85	William Davis
1985	Frank Miller
1985-87	Larry Grossman
1987-90	Andy Brant (interim)
1990-	Mike Harris
Liberals	
Until 1942	Mitchell Hepburn
1942-43	Gordon Conant
1943-44	Harry Nixon
1944-45	Mitchell Hepburn
1945-48	Farquhar Oliver (interim)
1948-51	Walter Thompson
1951-58	Farquhar Oliver (interim)
1958-63	John Wintermeyer
1963-64	Farquhar Oliver (interim)
1964-67	Andy Thompson
1967-76	Robert Nixon
1976-82	Stuart Smith
1982-90	David Peterson
1990-91	Robert Nixon (interim)
1991	Murray Elston (interim)
1991-92	Jim Bradley (interim)
1992-96	Lyn McLeod
1996-	Dalton McGuinty
NDP	
Until 1942	No leader
1942-53	E.B. Joliffe
1953-70	Donald C. MacDonald
1970-78	Stephen Lewis
1978-82	Michael Cassidy
1982-96	Bob Rae
1996	Bud Wildman (interim)
1996-	Howard Hampton

view about what is appropriate and acceptable in the practice of government, it follows that when the government is re-elected the opposition is defeated. Table 3 reminds us of who the players were following the Robarts era. This information may be useful in trying to understand more clearly what has happened to Ontario since 1971. It seems obvious, for example, that part of the reason why Bill Davis survived was that neither of his opponents appeared to meet the leadership requirements of the Ontario political culture. Neither had been tested in public office at the provincial level — one of the prices opposition parties pay for long-serving administrations from one party — and each had weaknesses that may have undermined his ability to look like a premier-in-waiting. Stephen Lewis was a brilliant public speaker who was enormously effective in the legislature in opposition. But, unlike most politicians, he spoke in sentences, an ability so uncommon that it actually frightens people. He was "too clever by half" — a trait that easily translates into arrogance in the minds of ordinary voters. Bob Nixon, on the other hand, had a mercurial temper that sometimes appeared as a kind of petulance. As a result the many excellent qualities of both men were lost to sight, and Bill Davis was able to carry on.

It is of course to his credit that Davis finally accepted the electorate's judgement and learned how to manage the circumstances of minority government with great skill. But there is some evidence that the inclination to arrogance remained, even if it was later replaced, for public consumption, by the famous indecision. Even if the need for a gloved hand in the legislature was obvious, Davis remained dominant and authoritarian with his cabinet. Every civil servant has an illustration of this — mine comes from the struggle over the passage of the bill to create a new municipality in the Thirty Thousand Islands of Georgian Bay. This was not a measure of great consequence to the government (although a number of its close friends were directly affected by it), and, when the bill got into trouble in the legislature's ongoing scrap between the Liberals and the NDP, with the end of the 1979 session only days away, the government decided to drop it. At the last minute a compromise requiring the government to accept the NDP's help (but also promising an Ontario version of "dishing the Whigs") was found. Early on the morning of the final day of the session, the premier convened what can only be described as a political cabinet, where the bill's principal citizen backer made the case to proceed. Davis then put the question to his colleagues (nearly every major minister was present at the time) and when every single one of them said the measure should stay dropped, he announced that he was glad everyone had agreed that the compromise should proceed.[11]

By this time, of course, the character of the leadership struggle had changed quite dramatically. Nixon decided to step down as Liberal leader in 1976 and was replaced by Stuart Smith, whose detached intellectual manner starkly contrasted with the electorate's notion of either a leader of the opposition or a premier. After the NDP's failure in 1977 to build on the position achieved in 1975, Stephen Lewis also stepped aside and was replaced by Michael Cassidy at a 1978 convention. In a perverse way, these changes broke another kind of connection that many might regard as significant. Although Nixon remained in the legislature and later became a member of the Peterson cabinet, his departure from the leadership removed from the centre of things a man with an encyclopedic knowledge of Ontario's history borne of his family's long years of service to the progressive cause. Stephen Lewis had a similar background on the left, not just through his father, but also through his brother and sisters, who had worked for many years in the backrooms of the NDP and the CCF (Co-operative Commonwealth Federation).[12]

But while there can be little doubt that these changes, by the end of the 1970s, altered the nature of the political contest by substituting two comparatively weak leaders of the opposition parties for the strength that had gone before, it remains clear that the Ontario electorate continued to turn up its nose at the quality of the Davis leadership. Perhaps the most striking evidence for this reaction is found in the data for the 1981 election (see Table 2). This was the occasion, as the press trumpeted at the time, when the Conservatives "recovered" their majority. For months afterwards, the premier deflected criticism in the legislature by inviting the opposition to remember the "realities of March 19th" (the date of the 1981 election).

In fact, what actually happened in 1981 was that the Conservative vote — expressed as a percentage share of the registered electorate — did not change at all from 1977. Instead, the NDP lost six percentage points (nearly a third of its 1977 vote) to abstentions, apparently because of enormous dissatisfaction with the leadership of Michael Cassidy,[13] and that guaranteed the Tories their majority by giving them several seats through the default of a missing NDP vote. The Liberals lost a further two percentage points from the relatively strong position they had enjoyed in 1975, and the result was that lacklustre opposition leadership, not a new wave of popular approval for the Conservatives, was the deciding factor.

All of this suggests that the Conservative loss in the 1985 election was as much due to Bill Davis's record since 1971 as it was to the obvious ineptitude of Frank Miller. In retrospect, it was almost as if the province was simply waiting for someone (although not quite anyone) to restore the kind of deliberate and decisive management of the province's affairs to which the people had become accustomed before 1971. These sentiments may well have been encouraged by the premier's behaviour in the more secure conditions provided by the Tories' having recovered control of the legislature. Some trace of the old arrogance appeared again from time to time — most notably in the decision to advance full public funding to the Roman Catholic separate-school system without consulting either his cabinet or his caucus. There is little evidence that this policy affected the 1985 vote in any tangible way,[14] but the manner in which the decision was made likely added to the very substantial memory of Conservative insensitivity under Bill Davis. Once again, the question of appropriate leadership seems to lie at the root of understanding the changes that were taking place in Ontario politics.

The Interregnum — 1985–1995

The opportunity for change brought about by Davis's decision to resign therefore held the possibility of a renewal that might have preserved the Conservative party's domination of Ontario. These hopes were dashed completely when the leadership convention held early in 1985 picked Frank Miller for the job. Part of the problem was a decision by the party executive to cut off voting memberships as of the date of Davis's retirement announcement, thereby precluding the introduction of new blood into the process and ultimately leaving the convention largely in the hands of people not as broadly representative of the province as had been the case in the past.[15] At the same time, it appears probable that by delaying his resignation — had he followed the pattern established by his predecessors, he would have stepped down in 1981 or 1982 — Davis closed the door for possible candidates who were more likely to have met Ontario's leadership requirements than those who finally ran.[16]

Be that as it may, Miller very quickly showed that he was not going to be able to do the job. He started by unloading all the wise people who had been responsible for the Conservative party's successful electoral organization throughout the Davis years and found advisers who, to put it simply, ill understood the character of Ontario political life. (In contrast, fourteen years earlier, Davis began by bringing on board immediately the people who had run his opponent's campaign.) Miller's advisers in turn discovered that they had little confidence in their chief and proceeded to conduct an election campaign in which their leader was kept out of sight as much as possible and when in sight was actively prevented from answering questions — even from debating the other two leaders on television. There could hardly have been a more blunt statement of Miller's lack of leadership capacity, and very quickly the Tories began to pay the price.[17]

At the same time, as if by magic, an opposition leader who looked as if he could fill the void appeared. A transformed David Peterson, minus the metal-rimmed eyeglasses and five-o'clock shadow, dressed in appropriate grey slacks and jacket (to say nothing of red jogging suits), and possessed of a new capacity for public speaking, burst upon the campaign trail. The contrast with Frank Miller was electric. Immediately after the leadership convention, as the 1985 election campaign was about to begin, the Conservatives had an enormous lead in the polls, sitting at 56 per cent of the decided electorate, compared to 18 percent for the Liberals and 20 per cent for the NDP.[18] By the final week of the campaign this advantage had been entirely lost, with the margin shifting to a four-point lead for the Liberals.[19] In the end, the slight Conservative edge in seats proved irrelevant, and after the defeat of the government in the legislature, the Liberals, supported by the accord they had made with the NDP, took office.

It has frequently been observed that the principal value of this accord is that it provided the new Liberal government with a program — an agenda for government that they might not otherwise have had, if for no other reason than that David Peterson was almost as slow at decision-making as Bill Davis had been.[20] But the period of the accord contrasted with what had gone before. It was a time of good yet cautious management and, perhaps more importantly, of an attempt to restore the balance among the interests in terms of progressive legislation. The reward was the massive Liberal victory of 1987.

The new majority, however, brought a return to complacency, while the premier pursued Meech Lake. But governments who have decided to stop caring about the people and who call unnecessary elections do not sit well with an electorate that asks only for orderly management. More than any other factor, the inability of the Liberals to provide a satisfactory explanation for the early election call in 1990 croded their strength and ultimately deprived them of control of the campaign. At the outset they had an apparently decisive lead in the polls of 48 per cent of the decided electorate, against 31 per cent for the NDP and 21 per cent for the Conservatives.[21] By election day, just as had happened to Frank Miller, the Liberal lead had all been lost.

With the Conservatives now floundering in their attempt to find a leader to restore the party's standing, the electorate turned to the NDP as the only tolerable alternative. In this analysis, however, it is surely important to note that the NDP victory was as much due to accidents of support distribution as to any general welling-up of popular support. After all, as any observer of the modern Ontario system knows, when a party such as the NDP wins nearly every seat in southwestern Ontario, something somewhere has come unstuck[22] — and in any case, 37.6 per cent of the popular vote ought not to produce a legislative majority. At the same time, it needs to be recognized that Rae did appear to follow in a tradition admired generally by the province while both of his opponents quite clearly did not.

That these sentiments dominated at the time seems borne out by the reception accorded the Rae government by the Ontario electorate in the early months. The first Gallup poll after the election (taken in October 1990) gave the NDP 58 per cent of the decided vote — interestingly, that was precisely the level of support reached by the Harris government when it took office, according to an Angus Reid poll[23] — and support continued around that level (reaching 60 per cent in January 1991) until the following April. In February 1991 Gallup reported an approval rating for the premier himself of 70 per cent. It was obvious, in other words, that the Ontario people were happily willing to give the NDP a chance.

Then came the infamous budget of April 29, 1991 — the one the press said would send the province to the poorhouse — and the government's stock began to plummet. Within a month the Liberals had overtaken the NDP in the polls, and by July the premier's approval rating had dropped to 28 per cent. The party never recovered from that initial shock, and even the most cautious gambler could comfortably have wagered that the party would not win the next election. It was clear that there was no possibility of recovery.

It is easy to see that the NDP made the classic mistake of social democratic parties almost everywhere. Its task was not to take the opportunity of sudden power to give some life to sixty years of built-up expectations. Its mission should not have been to carry out even minor reforms — arguably it did not have a mandate to do anything even remotely radical — but rather to prove that it knew how to govern. The NDP needed to do what the Swedish social democrats did in the 1930s as they began their long period in office, or what the CCF did in Saskatchewan in 1944 — that is, govern competently and cautiously. Even if the party had won a massive victory (in terms of the vote) in 1990, this strategy would likely have been necessary. No doubt such a course would have meant apparently abandoning many of their most cherished aims, but the prize might well have been a more firmly based triumph in 1994 or 1995 and the chance to make a real start on a program of major change.

But that is not what happened, and so the NDP failed two tests of leadership: the one peculiar to all new parties in government, and the other central to Ontario's experience over the years. It would be difficult for even the most ardent partisan to claim that running up the provincial debt shows a capacity for competent management. There is some evidence as well that the government was perceived to have violated the fair-play requirements that appear to be part of the province's political culture, not only with the Social Contract but also with measures nominally designed, for example, to promote equal opportunity in employment. It was about as clear a case as Ontarians are likely to see of the adage that opposition parties do not win elections so much as governments lose them.

The 1995 Election and Beyond

In the end, most people in Ontario had little difficulty in deciding how to vote in the 1995 election. Confronted with two demonstrably unsuitable leaders, they turned to the only one who looked and sounded as if he knew what he was doing.

Bob Rae and the NDP had clearly shown their inability to manage the province properly, and by the middle of the campaign Lyn McLeod seemed little better. She had won the Liberal leadership early in 1992 by a narrow margin over Murray Elston, whom many observers thought was more suited to the job.[24] But even with the best will in the world she seemed unable to muster that combination of genuine caring and decisiveness that is expected in Ontario. As more and more people had a chance to see her in action, they appeared less impressed, and once again her party snatched defeat from the jaws of victory. On the eve of the 1995 campaign, an Environics poll gave the Liberals a lead that was even more commanding than the one they had had at the start of the 1990 campaign (and one they had enjoyed more or less continuously since the middle of 1991): 51 per cent of the decided electorate, to 25 per cent for the Conservatives and 21 per cent for the NDP. But barely a month later they were already trailing the Conservatives by four points.[25] By election day they would be crushed.

But if this is a fair account of events, it can hardly be said that Mike Harris and the Conservative party won the 1995 election because the people of Ontario have given up on their roots and turned overnight into mean-spirited and selfish individualists who have forgotten the plight of their fellow citizens. On the contrary, it looks as though they were trying to do what they have always done — pick the best leader available to manage the affairs of the province for the next four or five years. It is true, of course, that the Conservative program called for some rather Draconian changes to the status quo. But before everyone jumps to the conclusion that the Tories' victory signals a sea change in the values that have for ages dominated Ontario politics, some careful reflection is in order.

At least three kinds of observations may be made. First, it is simplistic to interpret what are essentially only changes in policy flowing from different attitudes and opinions rather than from new concepts of right and wrong, as heralding the dawn of a new age. The rightward shift in opinion now evident in much of North America is hardly the first of its kind, even in the second half of the twentieth century, and is no more likely to last than earlier shifts. It may simply be that the Conservative party's right wing has for the time being won control of its machinery, as it nearly did in 1971 when Bill Davis was chosen leader by a hair's breadth, or as it literally did in 1985, only to be thwarted by a Liberal leader who was more attractive than the Conservative leader.

Second, we cannot forget that we live, after all, in a capitalist society, in which selfishness has always been the basic motivating value, however much we may think we have been able to moderate its influence. It is worth remembering, as well, that it is easy to care for others when we are well off and times are good, but it is more difficult when times are bad. Perhaps "red toryism" in Ontario has actually been a product of the province's continued financial strength over the years since Confederation. In 1995, in the midst of a difficult financial crisis, it was not hard to forget one's neighbours, and it is not very surprising that the Ontario people appear to have forgotten their heritage. But if they did, this neglect is just as likely as not to be temporary. The roots of values such as caring and sharing lie as much in contemporary economic and social circumstances as do the roots of those values we Ontarians are told have replaced them and, in any case, no set of fundamental political values could disappear as quickly as the apostles of the new age claim.

Those considerations lead naturally to the third observation. The Conservatives were supported by 28 per cent of the registered electorate in 1995. In both 1987 and 1990 they had the support of 15 per cent. It seems reasonable to assume that those 15 per cent were dyed-in-the-wool Conservative voters who were unwilling to leave their party at any time. They were not won over in 1995 by the Common Sense Revolution; they were going to be there anyway. It is possible that the other 13 per cent who came on board in 1995 were won over by the Harris plan for the province, but that is hardly a sufficient base on which to build an entirely new view of what drives the Ontario political culture.

Therefore, as Ontarians approach the end of the century, the electorate continues to do what it has always done: reject incompetence and reward managerial skill. Ontarians were cross with Bill Davis for his indecision, but the alternatives were either worse or too frightening to contemplate, so the election merely resulted in a pair of minority legislatures. But once he had regained his majority — perversely, due to an even worse NDP leader — Davis was ready to make way for a successor. His party's choice — Frank Miller — was transparently foolish, and it came just as David Peterson was learning how to transform himself into the attractive political leader he became. Is it any wonder that the changes of the 1980s occurred?

And when confidence in the new team faltered, without any recovery on the Conservative side, the Ontario people turned to Bob Rae. This was not very surprising, given their preoccupation with the need for suitable leadership. They most explicitly did not turn to the NDP — the thinness of the vote shows that. Instead, they opted for the possibility that Bob Rae could fill the management void. For reasons not yet altogether clear, he could not pass the test either, and he and his party paid the price that was paid by his immediate predecessors.

So, too, will Mike Harris and the reformed Conservatives pay the price if they continue to act as though leadership means telling other people what to do without any discussion. They will be respected if they are seen to be managing the province; they may even be admired for sticking to the guns they laid out in their election manifesto. But there are two sides to the Ontario political culture, and if the new government is perceived to be overstepping the bounds of fairness and propriety set out by those other values, which have been every bit as important over the years as the more prominent demand for managerial efficiency, it will suffer. Already there is some evidence of that happening. An April 1997 poll gave the Conservatives only 35 per cent of the decided electorate, a considerable decline from their post-election high, with the Liberals at 39 per cent and the NDP at 17 per cent.[26]

In short, it does appear to be the same old Ontario. There is a very striking, yet simple, thread that runs through this analysis and that binds it together. It may not be too much to say that the inability of the principal political parties — whether in government or opposition — to pick the right leaders has more to do with the character of political life in the province than anything else. But people have been saying that for years.

Endnotes

1. The concept of the political culture, which had an elementary simplicity in its original formulation, has been turned inside out by analysts over the years. There is a great deal to be said for looking again at what it was supposed to mean. See Gabriel A. Almond and Sidney Verba, *The Civic Culture*, Princeton NJ: Princeton University Press, 1963.
2. The ideas in this paragraph are drawn from S.J.R. Noel, *Patrons, Clients, Brokers: Ontario Society and Politics, 1791–1896*, Toronto: University of Toronto Press, 1990, 232–3.
3. S.F.Wise, "The Ontario Political Culture: A Study in Complexities," in *God's Peculiar Peoples: Essays on Political Culture in Nineteenth Century Canada*, Ottawa: Carleton University Press, 1993, 215.
4. John Wilson, "The Red Tory Province: Reflections on the Character of the Ontario Political Culture," in Donald C. MacDonald, ed., *The Government and Politics of Ontario*, 2nd ed., Toronto: Van Nostrand Reinhold, 1980, 208–225.
5. Wilson, "The Red Tory Province," 225.
6. The passage of time has allowed us to forget that Bill Davis was by no means the party's runaway choice that many of his predecessors had been — he finally won the job from Allan Lawrence on the fourth ballot by a margin of only 44 votes out of 1,580 cast. Lawrence was widely regarded as the leader of the more right-wing elements in the party, a portent of things to come later.
7. The Conservatives won 51 seats in 1975, 58 in 1977, and 52 in 1985 (in all three cases, there were 125 seats in the legislature).

8. The leader of the Liberal party, Bob Nixon, in 1975 was willing to arrange a combination that might overthrow the government, but he could not get his caucus colleagues to agree. Part of the difficulty was the distance in the opposition parties' respective seat strengths from the Conservatives', but the real problem was the fact that Stephen Lewis, as the leader of the largest opposition party, would almost certainly have become premier. (Letter to the author from Bob Nixon, March 27, 1996.) In 1977, Nixon was no longer Liberal leader, but had an approach been made then, it is probable that Lewis would have rejected it. Rosemary Speirs reports that Lewis was initially hostile to the idea that the NDP should support the Liberals following the 1985 election. See Speirs, *Out of the Blue: The Fall of the Tory Dynasty in Ontario*, Toronto: Macmillan, 1986, 136.
9. Quoted in Speirs, *Out of the Blue*, 5.
10. In fact, the government only notified the opposition house leaders of its intention to treat the pending vote as a matter of confidence minutes before it was to take place.
11. Every student of parliamentary government knows that this sort of thing happens from time to time even if these occasions are not always documented. There are several sources for this story to whom I have promised anonymity. I can say, however, that they include several senior civil servants whose advice had been called upon at the time to draft the necessary amendments for presentation later that day in the legislature.
12. There are many kinds of historical connections. It would be remiss not to mention that Michael Cassidy's father was one of the principal authors of the Regina Manifesto and later a candidate for the leadership of the Ontario Liberal party.
13. Even though Cassidy retained his Ottawa seat, reports of workers in the field throughout the campaign were rife with stories of voter dissatisfaction, especially among party members, which meant a weakened capacity to mount major campaigns in the constituencies.
14. There was nonetheless some effect. See Speirs, *Out of the Blue*, 118–119.
15. Speirs, *Out of the Blue*, 35.
16. A number of such people — for example, Robert Elgie — had left the government for other pursuits by the time of the 1985 convention, and even some who had not, such as Roy McMurtry, had to be persuaded almost at the last minute even to consider running.
17. A very thorough account both of the internal errors of judgement and organization and the mismanagement of the election campaign can be found in Speirs, *Out of the Blue*, 80–128.
18. Speirs, *Out of the Blue*, 92.
19. Speirs, *Out of the Blue*, 122.
20. See, in particular, the account of life in the Liberal government in the period after 1987 in Georgette Gagnon and Dan Rath, *Not Without Cause: David Peterson's Fall from Grace*, Toronto: Harper Collins, 1991.

21. Gagnon and Rath, *Not Without Cause*, 113. Gagnon and Rath describe in fascinating detail the indecision and bickering that dogged the Liberal campaign team throughout the 1990 election.
22. A moment's examination of the very small margins of victory in a number of constituencies, to say nothing of success in areas where the NDP had always had a poor showing, should have been enough to make clear to any observer how fragile the new government's position was.
23. *The Globe and Mail*, November 18, 1995.
24. The Ontario Liberal party seems to have had a difficult time over the years picking the right leader for the circumstances it confronted. Since 1934, it has had eighteen different leaders, including those who served only on an interim basis. In the same period the Conservatives have had ten leaders, and the CCF/NDP seven.
25. Angus Reid, December 1996. I am indebted to G.P. Murray and G.P. Murray Research Limited for enabling me to follow the standings of the Ontario parties since the beginning of 1994 through their poll-tracking service.
26. Angus Reid, April 1997 (reported in *The Globe and Mail*, May 9, 1997).

5

TV Advertising Campaigns in the 1995 Ontario Election

Robert MacDermid

This chapter poses a number of basic questions about political campaign advertising on television.[1] Most studies of Canadian election campaigns by academics have paid little attention to the effect of ad campaigns on election outcomes.[2] Given the difficulty of ascertaining the importance and the effect of ad campaigns, it is hardly surprising that the topic has often been conveyed through insider accounts that are undoubtedly coloured by partisanship and self-interest. The lack of systematic knowledge of ad campaigns is perhaps best reflected in the inability of scholars to say, with any certainty, whether such advertising has any effect on the end result. Certainly there are boosters, mostly those with a professional interest, but the evidence is too easily undermined, and the prospect of coming up with a research design that could study the effects of advertising free from experimental effects and in a true election environment is still distant and possibly nonexistent.[3] Yet even if we as researchers cannot arrive at a conclusive answer about the effect of advertising on voters, we may still address a number of questions that relate to the dimensions of ad campaigns, such as where and when ads run, how much advertising campaigns cost, and how the parties build advertising strategies. In the end, these sorts of questions may turn out to be more important than the "effect" question.

Television advertising has become the most important way that political parties communicate with voters during election campaigns. The political spot permits the campaign manager, video producer,

Table 4 Campaign Period Expenditures, 1985-95						
	1995			1990		
	Lib	NDP	PC	Lib	NDP	PC
Advertising	45%	41%	68%	49%	53%	41%
Travel	13%	17%	13%	9%	17%	13%
Fundraising	0%	2%	2%	8%	3%	7%
Research & polling	9%	7%	2%	19%	7%	4%
Office	14%	9%	8%	7%	3%	4%
Salaries & consulting	0%	10%	3%	0%	6%	0%
Transfers	5%	3%	3%	2%	6%	1%
Other	14%	11%	2%	6%	6%	30%
Total $	2,789,323	2,528,343	2,585,625	2,987,138	1,624,810	2,402,159

	1987			1985		
	Lib	NDP	PC	Lib	NDP	PC
Advertising	50%	48%	54%	43%	59%	49%
Travel	9%	14%	9%	7%	12%	14%
Fundraising	0%	9%	6%	6%	8%	5%
Research & polling	16%	4%	9%	8%	3%	11%
Office	6%	3%	5%	8%	2%	9%
Salaries & consulting	4%	12%	3%	8%	13%	6%
Transfers	9%	6%	1%	5%	3%	1%
Other	5%	4%	12%	14%	0%	6%
Total $	2,597,785	1,475,423	1,974,702	1,596,235	1,353,198	4,262,845

and candidate a degree of control over the message that would be impossible to achieve in face-to-face communication. By rehearsing the message, altering facial expressions, changing text, inserting stock shots, and so on, the producers can control the final product in a way that would simply be impossible for even the best public speaker. Equally important, television ads can reach enormous audiences and recite the message to them over and over again. So long as there is uncertainty about the effect of advertising and how it works, it is clearly best to buy as much air time as possible and repeat the message as often as possible. This preference for television advertising over other forms of campaign communication has transformed the way parties operate and campaign. Not only do they dedicate scarce financial and organizational resources to ad campaigns over other uses, but the campaign as reported in the media and discussed in the electorate increasingly revolves around the battle between thirty-second spots. Political dialogue has to some extent been reduced to exchanges between spots.

The growing significance of television advertising to election campaigns is reason enough to initiate a systematic study of campaign advertising and to begin to build a body of information that can substantiate or undermine the claims of supporters of political dialogue through advertising. Although parties are secretive about the details of their advertising campaigns, and those who work in the industry zealously protect information about the business, there are nevertheless some valuable sources of data available to researchers. This chapter uses those data to provide answers to some basic questions about the dimensions of political advertising campaigns in the context of the landmark election of a Conservative government in the 1995 Ontario provincial election.

Election scholarship lacks much of the basic documentation concerning how many ads run, which stations run ads, how frequently, at what times, during which programs ads appear, how much air time costs, how big the audience is, and so on. This chapter addresses some of these questions as the first step in understanding the importance of television ads to election campaigns. A basic description of ad campaigns not only is important in attempting to assess the effect of ads on voters, but it also tells us something about the campaign itself. Knowing the number of ads each party ran tells us something about campaign strategy and campaign finances. Knowing when the ads ran tells us something about different buying strategies and target groups, and knowing the progression of ads through the campaign

tells us something about how issues developed and changed throughout the campaign.

The Data

The information used in the chapter is drawn from five different
sources. First, to answer questions about the numbers of ads, the
stations on which they ran, the cost of air time, and so on, the station
logs made available by the Canadian Radio-television and Telecom-
munications Commission (CRTC)[4] for eleven channels were analyzed. The stations, listed in Table 6, represent over a third of the
thirty Ontario-based stations on air in June 1994. The stations were
chosen to reflect region, channel ownership, and affiliation, as well
as population density. The CRTC logs contain entries for all programming, including commercials. All privately owned channels are
required to keep programming logs, and many CBC channels keep
these logs as well, although they are not required to do so. The logs
tell how often each party advertised between May 17 and June 6, in
which programs the ads ran, at what time the ads ran, how long the
ads were, which stations ran the ads, and which ads received air time
at different points in the campaign and during the day.

The second source of data is the Bureau of Broadcast Measurement (BBM) survey for June 1 to 14, 1995. This quarterly survey of
audience sizes coincides almost exactly with the election campaign
and provides a basis for estimating audience sizes and therefore the
effectiveness of media buying strategies.

The third data source is the ads themselves. The parties supplied
copies of all of the ads they ran during the campaign, providing a
base to answer questions about campaign strategy and issues, as well
as offering insight into production values and the costs of producing
the ads.

The fourth source of information was interviews with members of
the campaign teams[5] and with advertising creators and buyers in the
industry. Interviewers were able to speak with most of the key figures
in the Liberal, PC and NDP campaigns about the course of the
campaign and particularly about the advertising campaign.

Finally, data on campaign expenditures for the 1995 Ontario election reveal some important differences in strategy across parties and
in the extent to which parties have come to rely on television advertising.

The Dimensions of the Ad Campaign

How much did the parties spend on television advertising? The parties' expense reports for the campaign period give a fairly accurate indication of expenditures in different areas of the campaigns. Unfortunately, the reports are not sufficiently detailed to answer all questions about advertising expenditures during and prior to the campaign. The reports do indicate sums paid for advertising, but they do not indicate how these totals break down into production costs and air time. Most of the ads in the 1995 campaign appear to have been low-budget efforts, and this suggests that most of the advertising funds must have been spent on air time. It is also difficult to determine what percentage of total advertising expenditures was spent in the pre-election period. It is likely that some small percentage of production costs would have been incurred prior to the election period.

Table 4 shows a breakdown of campaign expenditures for each party for the past four Ontario general elections. Throughout this ten-year period, advertising has consumed close to half of all campaign expenditures for all parties in all campaigns. The lowest expenditure was 41 per cent, spent by the NDP in 1995 and the PC party in 1990. The highest total was 68 per cent, spent by the PC party in its winning 1995 campaign. It should be noted that prior to campaign expenditure reforms, the PC party spent over $2 million on advertising in its losing 1985 campaign — a figure that has yet to be topped. The table also illustrates a couple of differences between parties that are related to their organization and ideology. As the party of the working class, the NDP has spent much greater percentages of its campaign expenditures on salaries than is the case for the other two parties. The NDP has always maintained a large organization and focused on mobilization strategies that are particularly suited to its working-class electoral base. Getting out the vote through door-to-door canvassing has always been a reputed strength of the NDP and usually requires greater organizational expenses and paid staff. By contrast, the Liberal and PC parties appear to have relied on services donated by those who could afford to work for the party when needed. The table also reveals some differences between the parties in expenditures on research and polling. Some of these differences are the result of the timing of expenditures. For example, the small PC expenditure on polling during the 1995 election does not include a large precampaign poll the Tories used to plan their election strategy.

The importance of advertising costs in overall campaign expenditures underlines the prominence of campaign advisers who control and guide these expenditures. Key advisers and creators of the campaign come from the advertising world. They are ad producers, advertising researchers, media buyers, image consultants, and pollsters. Their language and concerns are about audience sizes and demographics, camera angles, staged campaign events, and the purchase of advertising time. To a large extent, it is these people who manage the campaign and who determine what policies are marketed and how they are sold. In one sense, people with these abilities have always had the ear of the powerful. Image consultants and public opinion specialists are nothing new to politics. But in a new way, they have brought into campaigns the technical language and concerns of advertising and persuasion over what has, perhaps questionably, been thought to be traditional public policy and ideological concerns. At the very least, making advertising the most important part of a campaign crowds out other forms of discussion of issues.

How often did the parties advertise? There does not appear to be any research that systematically shows how often parties advertised during a campaign.[6] The widely held and incorrect assumption seems to be that campaign advertising legislation dictates the air time of the parties and keeps it roughly equal or at least reflective of the parties' share of seats in the legislature. But in fact, there is no such legislation. In Ontario there are no requirements that paid television time be apportioned according to some formula for fairness. In reality, there are only two limits on the air time a party can buy during an election: the number of advertising spots available and the party's advertising budget. The current legislation leaves the parties free to determine their own mix of election spending. As will become clear below, there are good reasons to question this free-handed approach, for in reality, it allows some parties to monopolize the air time of particular stations, effectively shutting out the ads of other parties.

An analysis of the logs from the sample of eleven stations reveals some large differences in the ad campaigns of the three main parties in the June 1995 Ontario provincial election. As Table 5 shows, of the 2,640 campaign commercials aired on the eleven stations between May 17 and June 6, PC ads made up 53 per cent of the total, surpassing the Liberal party, which would take second place in the election, by 2 to 1 and the incumbent NDP by almost 3 to 1. When

Table 5
Number and Length of TV Ads by Party
in the 1995 Ontario Election

		%	15 sec.	30 sec.	Mins	%
			Length		Total	
Liberals	701	26.6	5	696	349.25	27.2
Consevatives	1407	53.3	2	1405	703	54.8
NDP	493	18.7	145	348	210.25	16.4
Family Coal.	39	1.5	0	0	19.5	1.5
	2640	100	152	2488	1282	100.0

the numbers of ads are translated into minutes of air time, the NDP disadvantage is magnified: it trailed the Conservatives by 3.3 to 1 and the Liberals by 1.7 to 1 while the Liberals trailed the Conservatives by 2 to 1.

Without comparable data from other elections, it is difficult to interpret these ratios and place them in the perspective of past elections. Certainly, the Conservatives had a very decisive edge in air time and numbers of spots. But whether this edge translated into advertising effectiveness is difficult to determine. While those in the advertising business and especially those selling media space like to cite the credo that "advertising is like manure — the more you spread it, the better it is," there is little hard evidence on the effectiveness of repeating ads. However, it is assumed that the more often a message is repeated, the more likely it is to make an impression. Of course, in the case of real-world advertising, this assumption is obviously false since many products fail regardless of the frequency of their advertising messages. Furthermore, it is uncertain whether the Conservative advantage in numbers of spots translates into an advantage in the size of the viewing audience. If the Conservative ads ran on stations with smaller viewing audiences, then it is still conceivable that NDP and Liberal ads could have been seen by as many people as viewed the Conservative ads. But this does not address questions about ad targeting, both across regions and during the viewing day. For example, a few ads aired during prime time might be seen by a larger audience than many ads run during daytime shows. Furthermore, it is likely that the parties will target particular clusters of voters who are most likely to support their views and buy air time to cover those geographic and demographic groups.

It is apparent from comments by campaign organizers that the Tories placed enormous importance on the TV advertising campaign. As one organizer put it, the role of the advertising campaign "was to drive the message, to drive up the awareness of the contrast, that we're the agents of change with clear policies, and to drive the contrasts between us and the Liberal positions."[7] Leslie Noble, the Conservative campaign manager, underlined the importance the Tories placed on the ad campaign:

In any campaign, advertising is fundamental; it is the only means ... you have to get your message out to the population, unfiltered by the media. Any media report has whatever bias that may be built in, it's not an unfiltered message, whereas paid advertising is unfiltered because it gets straight to your marketplace as you want it delivered. We aimed for message market saturation in the weeks that we had for advertising, we really had three weeks, and we loaded the bulk of our money into that percentage-wise.[8]

Table 5 also shows that the NDP's ad campaign differed from the other two parties' with respect to the use of fifteen-second ads. The Liberals and the Conservatives used thirty-second spots almost exclusively, while 30 per cent of the NDP ads were shorter, fifteen-second spots. The cost of shorter spots is usually about 65 per cent of that of the longer spots, so from a cost perspective, the NDP strategy may not have been particularly efficient. If a strategy can be extracted, the NDP appears to have wanted to maximize the frequency of its spots while minimizing the content of the spots. But just as likely an explanation is the allocation of funds within the campaign. The NDP has a long history of focusing on building local campaigns and emphasizing volunteer campaign activities rather than relying solely on advertising. While volunteers may be free, their organization and training are certainly not, and it may be that the party preferred to allocate a larger portion of its campaign spending to these activities rather than to TV advertising. It should also be remembered that the NDP, despite being in government, carried a large debt from the 1990 campaign right up to the 1995 campaign. This must have affected the party's ability to spend on training and other traditional campaign activities in the lead up to the campaign and

Table 6 The Distribution of TV Ads by Station and Party in the 1995 Ontario Election					
	Lib.	PC	NDP	FC	TOTAL
CFPL London	84	94	21	0	199
%	(42)	(47)	(11)	(0)	(100)
CFTO Toronto	79	70	80	0	229
%	(35)	(31)	(35)	(0)	(100)
CHBX Sault Ste. M.	120	92	120	0	332
%	(36)	(28)	(36)	(0)	(100)
CHCH Hamilton	64	187	8	0	259
%	(25)	(72)	(3)	(0)	(100)
CHEX Peterborough	32	233	0	17	282
%	(11)	(83)	(0)	(6)	(100)
CHNB North Bay	28	8	17	0	53
%	(53)	(15)	(32)	(0)	(100)
CITY Toronto	128	57	64	0	249
%	(51)	(23)	(26)	(0)	(100)
CKCO Kitchener	51	207	102	22	382
%	(13)	(54)	(27)	(6)	(100)
CKPR Thunder Bay	39	31	42	0	112
%	(35)	(28)	(38)	(0)	(100)
CKVR Barrie	0	237	0	0	237
%	(0)	(100)	(0)	(0)	(100)
CKWS Kingston	76	191	39	0	306
%	(25)	(62)	(13)	(0)	(100)

resulted in the shifting of some of these expenses into the campaign period. It is also worth recalling that the Conservative party struggled with a large debt throughout the 1990s and entered 1994 more than $2 million in the red. This, however, does not seem to have affected the PCs' ability to raise funds during the campaign period.

Where did the parties advertise? To return to the practice of geographical ad targeting, the overall Conservative advantage in spots is both under- and overrepresented in Table 5's totals for all eleven stations. Table 6 shows that for several stations the advantage was many times more decisive.

At the extreme, the Conservatives controlled the entire political advertising inventory (the total of available spots) on CKVR (Barrie), a station that is carried by cable services in Toronto and especially in the outer areas of the Greater Toronto Area (GTA), the suburban and middle-class belt where the Conservatives gained seats from the Liberals and the NDP. They also had very large leads in the numbers of spots showing on CHCH (Hamilton), CHEX (Peterborough), CKCO (Kitchener), and CKWS (Kingston). The first three of these channels are also carried into the Toronto region by cable services. The Conservatives trailed both the Liberals and the NDP in spots showing on the two Toronto stations, CFTO and CITY. The relatively small amount of air time purchased by the Tories on CITY may have been a targeting decision, for viewers of CITY, with its youthful image, do not appear to be part of the Conservative electorate. CFTO is a slightly more complicated case, with the most expensive air time and, through the Baton-CTV system, a provincewide reach for some advertising spots. Advertising on CFTO will be examined in greater depth below.

Tables 5 and 6 suggest that the Conservative campaign had a very well considered media buying strategy. The Tories were able to buy relatively inexpensive air time on outlying stations and have the messages carried into Toronto and the suburban areas they had targeted as their potential electorate. In one case, loyal viewers of a channel would have seen nothing but Conservative party ads. This apparent strategic success (I remind the reader that the question of audience share is still left unanswered) must have been the result of careful geographical targeting of the party's potential electorate and the organization and speed of the media buy (the party's purchase of advertising spots). Since the NDP government had the luxury of setting the date of the election, it also had the advantage in placing its media buy. Interviews with campaign strategists suggest that this advantage was squandered. The Conservatives with the help of Jamie Watt, who in the words of one Liberal strategist "blew our doors off on the buy,"[9] began buying choice air time as soon as the election writ was issued. In some cases, this resulted in the other parties' being nearly or completely shut out through the purchase of the entire advertising inventory. Leslie Noble, the Conservative campaign manager, indicated the importance of the buying strategy and the speed with which it was carried out:

It was done the second the election was announced — we had our buy plan designed two months prior to the election so that it would be ready. Much of it is how much muscle and speed you can exert ... We designed our buy around the demographics we had to reach and where we thought we were going to get our biggest bang for our buck in terms of population, number of seats, and bought heavily in those areas.[10]

Alister Campbell, another key campaign worker, underlined the importance of the Conservative strategy:

We spent almost all of our money on the buy and we won the race on the buy. We ordered our ads hours before Rae called the election, the Liberals didn't get their buy in for another thirty-six hours, so we won almost all of the avails [unsold inventory of spots], we had better positioning, better placing and also we disproportionately weighted our campaign to the back end. In the final week, we operated on the assumption that the other two guys would be viciously negative against us so that we would be able to match their combined throw weight.[11]

The importance of media buying strategies to campaigns deserves some comment. Media buyers are agents acting between the media, who are selling advertising time or space, and the customer, who is selling a product. Buyers develop relationships with media sellers and often enter into contractual relationships to provide customers in return for reduced rates. Large and influential media buyers can offer customers reduced rates while guaranteeing sellers large blocks of sold time or space. Political parties may benefit from a relationship with a media buyer in terms of expertise and perhaps reduced rates. The Liberals have long had a close relationship with Vickers and Benson, and the media buy for the Liberals was done through Genesis, a company half-owned by Vickers and Benson. The Conservatives used Thomas Watt, a London-based buyer, and the NDP used Media Dimension.

When did the parties advertise? Table 7, showing the purchase of ads throughout the three-week advertising period, confirms Campbell's comment about the Conservative strategy of end-weighting the party's media buy: the Conservatives placed 43 per cent of their spots in the final week. The third week of advertising was also the Liberals' heaviest, but the NDP bought more time in the second week than in

Table 7			
1995 Ontario General Election: Loading of TV Ads on Eleven Channels over the Three-Week Advertising Period			
	WEEK		
	17-23/05	24-30/05	31/05-6/06	
Liberals %	33.8	27.5	38.7	100
N	(237)	(193)	(271)	701
Conservatives %	29.3	27.3	43.4	100
N	(412)	(384)	(611)	1407
NDP %	23.9	40.2	37.4	100
N	(118)	(198)	(177)	493

the final one. The NDP strategy contrasts sharply with those of the other two parties: not only was the NDP's effort in the first week small in comparison to those of the other two parties, but the NDP seemed to concentrate on the middle period of the campaign. Given the government's advantage in calling the election, the apparent ad buying strategy seems to reflect a degree of disorganization, which did not serve the party well. Alternately, it reflects a strategic calculation that had the party starting slow, coming on in the middle of the campaign, and finishing with the other parties. If that was the buying strategy, it turned out to be a failure in timing, weighting, and extent of the buy.

The Conservative buying strategy aimed to allow the PCs to run more ads in the last week of the campaign than the two other parties combined and thus gave them an enormous edge in being able to respond in force to any negative attacks that did develop, as well as in out-advertising the other parties during a period when many voters were making up their minds. Some of this edge in the final week must have been the result of slow media buying by the Liberal party and the NDP. One can only assume that given the direction of the campaign, the NDP and the Liberals would have liked to have bought many more spots in the final week, but much of the available time had already been booked by the Conservatives. In the final week, the Conservatives used attack ads against the Liberals and were able to match the frequency of attacks from the other parties. In retrospect, the Tory buying strategy showed brilliant campaign management. The party always had enough choice spots to both get

its message across in the early going and defend itself against negative attacks once it had reached the front of the pack.

How often did specific ads run and when? Television ad campaigns in Canada, short as they are in comparison to American
campaigns, still permit parties to run several series of different ads
according to precampaign strategies and midcampaign corrections.
All of the parties changed their ads as the campaign wore on. This
was especially true for the Liberals and the NDP, who, finding
themselves falling behind the Conservatives, produced different and
tougher ads as the campaign progressed. As one NDP strategist put
it: "As we saw the quite dramatic shift in voter support from the Grits
to the Tories, clearly we had to move from this gentle doubt-raising
about the capacity of Lyn McLeod to be premier and the capacity of
the Liberal party to govern, to a much more aggressive posture as it
was clear that the Liberals were dropping out of the race and the
Tories were moving ahead."[12]

Unfortunately not all of the station logs used in the analysis
listed the titles of the ads. CFTO, the flagship station of CTV, was
one of the few that did record titles for nearly all of the ads, and
Table 8 shows when new ads appeared and roughly for how long
they ran.

A number of things stand out in this table. First, the parties ran
a number of different ads: there were eight Liberal ads, seven NDP
ads, and six Conservative ads. The pattern of ads changes quite
dramatically across the three week-long periods in the campaign.
All of the parties tended to be more focused in the first week of
the campaign, when they were intent on stating their main campaign themes. The Conservatives hammered away with a single
ad attacking both "able-bodied welfare recipients" and "job quotas," clearly and repeatedly stating the difference between their
position on these issues and that of the Liberals. All of these ads
were cheaply produced from stills and were essentially compare-
and-contrast ads. Only one set of Conservative ads, "Vision,"
featured out-of-studio shots and displayed some sense of technical
expertise or production values. The Conservative strategy was a
mixture, preferring air time over production values but also using
stark ads to reinforce stark messages. In this sense, the ads were
not nearly as amateurish as they appeared. Strategists from all
three parties acknowledged the effectiveness of these ads in "driving a wedge into the electorate" on these issues. As one adviser
said, "the comparison ads on workfare and employment equity

Table 8			
Ads on CFTO by Party and Week in the 1995 Ontario Election			
	17-23/05	24-30/05	31/05-6/06
Liberals			
Action plan	17	4	
Experts/balanced budget	7	2	1
Irresponsible		1	10
Realistic			10
Reality — jobs	5		
Reality — jobs 2	3	2	1
Reality of jobs/youth		3	
Tightrope		11	
Missing			2
Conservatives			
Taxes		16	5
Vision			5
Vision-revised			5
Weathervane			13
Weathervane-revised			3
Welfare/quotas	25	7	3
Missing			1
NDP			
54%	2	6	2
Add up	2	6	2
Flags			7
Future			6
Health		13	3
Social contract	10		4
Taxes	3		
Missing	1		
Total	75	71	83

were great. They moved awareness of those issues up, they moved Harris's credibility up, and they moved the PC vote up. They were crucial in defining the issues of the campaign. They were superb. Not so much from a technical standpoint but [from] the understanding of how to use a wedge issue to define the campaign and to enhance your credibility in all of the places you need to be credible."[13]

In the early going, the NDP chose to defend its position on the Social Contract, a controversial set of agreements that, despite the opposition of the NDP's trade union supporters, decreased government spending through wage freezes and wage reductions rather than layoffs. In the eyes of some strategists, this decision was difficult to understand given the unpopularity of both the message and the messenger. The ads were mostly head-and-shoulder shots of Bob Rae explaining the Social Contract. They had higher production values than the Tory ads, but putting Rae front and centre was a questionable tactic given his unpopularity. Rosemary Barr, the NDP communications director, saw the ad "as a representation of the kind of decision that Bob and the government had to make over the course of the life of the government and the way in which those decisions were made that always kept people in mind ... That ad just resonated with people, that was our best one next to the American flag ad."14 Other strategists disagreed over the use of Rae in the early NDP ads: some thought it was the only possible tactic, while others thought the message unclear and the salesman less than enticing.

The strategy of the Liberal campaign in the first week was to sell the Red Book of election promises and to support it with endorsements from experts.

> For us, the role of the ad campaign was to reinforce the leader as a credible leader for the province and put her in somewhat of a premierlike setting and to reinforce change. We had three or four different ads where we talked about changing things and action-oriented things we'd do within thirty days, ninety days, one year, and whatever — and it was to show that we meant business, so that's what we were trying to project and do with our ad campaign.[15]

Even the Liberal strategy team realized that partly because of voters' lack of familiarity with the new party leader, Lyn McLeod, the message was fuzzy when compared to the hard-biting Harris ads. Liberal pollster Michael Marzolini ascribed the failure of the Liberal campaign to the leader's image:

The key driving motivator of votes was leadership during the entire campaign. The strategy was basically to take Lyn McLeod and make her into an authority figure, which was not easy. The initial ads were her sitting on a tightly buttoned tufted chair, and again we didn't have part of the execution. It was very clear that leadership was our Achilles' heel and also a prerequisite. You don't lead with your weakness in a campaign ...[16]

Week Two of the campaign saw all parties change their ad strategies. The Liberals, recognizing the surging Conservative support and the ineffectiveness of their first series of ads, shifted over to the attack, running the "Tightrope" ad, which suggested Tory tax cuts and spending cuts were enough to unbalance any tightrope walker. The general consensus on this attack ad was that it was confusing, and even Liberal strategists thought it ineffective:

The whole issue was that [Harris] was going too far. Unfortunately what we had was the mushy middle, but how can you make the balanced approach the preferred option? We didn't have the delivery mechanism in the party leader to give that credibility. The ad itself was seen as an interim measure until going with something more positive or more negative. It was targeting recent Liberal to PC switchers: it was looking at getting people to do the double take and think, "well suddenly we're electing a PC government right now. Gee, this is a little bit scary ... maybe we should go for something more balanced.[17]

The Liberal ads became even more negative in the final week, attacking the realism of the Conservative promises and the irresponsibility of the proposed tax cuts.

NDP ads in the second week also turned more negative, focusing on what were said to be inconsistencies in the Common Sense Revolution, the Conservative election platform, and injecting health care standards into the mix of issues. The beginning of Week Two must have made the NDP campaign team realize that the party's message was not getting across, and for the last two weeks the NDP ads became progressively more negative, ending with the "Flag" ad, which featured a Canadian flag merging into the Stars and Stripes as an indication of what was to come under a Tory government. At least for some observers, the "Flag" was thought to have helped the party recover from near annihilation. It is just as likely to have been seen as a last desperate attempt to play upon voters' fears of Americanization. Those fears either were overestimated by the NDP or were simply not credible coming from an unpopular government sinking in the polls as election day approached. Whether the "Flag" brought any new NDP voters or returned defectors to the fold is open to question. The ad's cynicism is just as likely to have assured one-time NDP voters in the correctness of their decision to desert the party in 1995.

The Conservative campaign responded to attacks from the Liberals with negative ads of its own in the final week. "Weathervane" was a low-budget effort (as were all Conservative ads but "Vision") that showed Liberal Leader Lyn McLeod as a weathervane that turned with every political breeze. The weathervane has a very long American political lineage, being used in many campaigns. It probably served to solidify the Conservative lead by bringing up, once again, doubts about McLeod's character and steadfastness. Certainly the ad was negative — even dirty politics — but no party was beyond that in the 1995 election.

When did the parties advertise during the viewing day? There are large and important differences in viewing audiences across the daily schedule of television programs. Not only do numbers of viewers change from program to program and from morning to afternoon to evening, but audience composition can vary greatly from show to show. Programming is targeted at specific audiences, and advertisers buy air time according to the size and sociodemographic characteristics of viewers. While product advertising often targets specific audiences, political advertising has a target audience of all viewers of voting age; that is, the sociodemographic characteristics of viewers are less important to political ad campaigns. However, there are still important factors for political advertisers to consider; cost is the most prominent but the broadcast coverage area and non-viewer-related characteristics of the programming also come into play.

The political spots placed on CFTO during the three-week campaign surface in a surprisingly small number of shows and time periods. Table 9 lists the shows during which the ads appeared and gives the estimated audience sizes from the June 1995 BBM survey. In Table 10, the shows are grouped, and the number of ads in each of the program groups is given by party for the three-week period of the advertising campaign.

Table 9: CFTO Programming Containing Political Advertising in the 1995 Ontario Election			
	Cost for 30 seconds		Audience Size
	Local	Province	
Movies			
BBS Late Movie		300	11,000
BBS Wednesday Movie	2,400		
Morning talk			
Canada A.M.		350	60,000
Dini		400	49,000
Live with Regis & Kathie Lee	1,300		127,000
Sitcom			
Cheers	450		60,000
Ellen	5,400	9,000	127,000
Full House	9,500		355,000
Home Improvement		20,000	298,000
Sports			
Indy 500	500		
Labatt's Blue Jays Baseball		5,700-11,000	350,000
Sports Beat Today	50		246,000
The Preakness Stakes	1,000		
Game shows			
Jeopardy	3,100		397,000
Wheel of Fortune		6,500	488,000
Network primetime shows			
Dr Quinn Medicine Woman	3,300	5,000	132,000
Lois & Clark	5,700	10,500	327,000
Melrose Place		19,000	158,000
News			
CTV News			288,000
Night Beat News	1,600		177,000
Night Beat at Dawn	50		15,000
World Beat News	2,400		418,000
Other			
1995 Daytime Emmy Awards	2,000		
Siskel & Ebert	100		31,000
The Bold and the Beautiful	450		64,000

Table 10
1995 Ontario Election:
Types of Programming in Which Ads Ran on CFTO

	Liberals		PC		NDP		Total	
	%	(N)	%	(N)	%	(N)	%	(N)
Game shows	09	(7)	7	(5)	21	(17)	13	(29)
Morning talk shows	32	(25)	28	(20)	18	(14)	26	(59)
Movies	0	(0)	8	(6)	4	(3)	4	(9)
Network primetime shows	5	(4)	6	(4)	1	(1)	4	(9)
News								
Evening	13	(10)	20	(14)	20	(16)	17	(40)
Late	0	(0)	19	(13)	15	(12)	11	(25)
Morning local	3	(2)	0	(0)	5	(4)	3	(6)
National	0	(0)	1	(1)	0	(0)	0	(1)
Total news	13%		40%		40%		31%	
Sitcom	25	(20)	4	(3)	1	(1)	10	(24)
Sports	10	(8)	4	(3)	13	(10)	9	(21)
Other	4	(3)	1	(1)	2	(2)	3	(6)
	100	(79)	100	(70)	100	(80)	100	229

News programs were the most frequent buy, containing 31 per cent of all party spots, and the 6:00 p.m. evening news slot was the most popular, containing 17 per cent of all of the ads. Within the news category, there was a considerable discrepancy: the NDP and the Conservatives placed 40 per cent of their ads in news programs, and the Liberals placed only 13 per cent of their ads in news programs. For a number of reasons, news programming is a highly valued advertising spot. Commercials in news programming take on the credibility of the newscast and, as was reported by one media seller, tend to be more believed by viewers. News programming is often promoted by emphasizing the journalistic experience of the news anchor and the credibility of the station's news gathering. Ads that run during this time apparently benefit from this "glow" of credibility. It should be no surprise that this type of programming would be a magnet for political advertising and that political advertising in turn should sometimes take on the form of a news broadcast.[18] But there are three other aspects of news programming that also contribute to its attraction to political advertising. First, news audiences tend to be very loyal, watching the same news show at the same time every day. This makes repeat advertising very effective since audience composition remains stable. Second, local news can be a very effective way of targeting a geographic area even when the station's signal is broadcast or carried by a cable service to a much greater area. As was mentioned above, the Conservatives bought heavily from the stations in the GTA. Although the signal is carried widely throughout the region, the CKVR news, for example, is probably most watched in the northern areas of the GTA, where, as it turned out, Conservative candidates were swept into office. Finally, news programming also has the virtue of having little audience duplication across the different daily newscasts. People tend to watch the news only once daily and at a specific time.[19] For all the above reasons, spots in news programming are especially valuable for political advertising. This explains why the NDP and the Conservatives placed by far the largest proportion of their ads in news programming. The Liberal buy is puzzling. It is difficult to say whether the Liberals had a conscious policy to buy in other time slots or, perhaps more likely, were simply shut out of this time period. The NDP and the Conservatives seem to have been quicker off the mark with their media buys and may have bought up most of the available news spots. By the time the Liberals were ready to purchase air time, most of the spots may have been sold, and available spots may have been in clusters with other parties' ads, making these spots less desirable. As a rule, stations do not like to sell and advertisers do not like to buy spots in advertising breaks that feature ads for competitors' products. As a result, the number of ad spots in an hour is reduced to the number of breaks in the program and not to the total ad time available in the hour. Only very occasionally do ads for different parties appear in the same program break, and this didn't happen during the entire ad campaign on CFTO.

After news programming, morning talk shows, *Canada A.M., Dini,* and *Live with Regis & Kathie Lee* were the most popular class of programs and time slots for party ads, containing 26 per cent of all ads. Once again there was some variation across parties in buying practices. The Liberals devoted a third of their ads to morning talk shows while the Conservatives were a close second at 28 per cent and the NDP followed with only 18 per cent of their spots in that time and class of programming. The heavy buy in talk shows by the Liberals may have been the result of their missing out on preferred news programming. Political campaigns suffer from a very short lead time, and advertising is at the mercy of available spot inventory. If political parties want to get their messages out to anyone, they may have to take what they can get. Morning talk shows represent a specific audience that has high loyalty but rather narrow demographics. The Conservatives, who had first choice of time slots, apparently thought this audience was less valuable than those of news or other programs such as game shows.

Game shows (*Jeopardy* and *Wheel of Fortune*), sitcoms (*Cheers, Ellen, Full House, Home Improvement*), sports (mostly Blue Jays baseball), and late local news all drew around 10 per cent each of the total party advertising. Once again there were some large differences: the NDP bought heavily (a three to one edge over the Conservatives) in game shows (perhaps fitting for a party that introduced casino gambling). The Liberals bought heavily in the sitcom category, placing 25 per cent of their advertising in this type of programming, while the other two parties tended to ignore it. Both game shows and sitcoms tend to have high audience loyalty combined with narrow demographics. Sports programming was popular with the Liberals and the NDP while late local news was favoured equally by the Conservative and NDP campaigns but shunned by the Liberals.

Network prime-time shows, with their large and diverse audiences, contained only 4 per cent of the spots. While they do not represent good vehicles for targeting specific audiences, they do attract very high ratings. Unfortunately for spending-capped political parties, they also contain the most expensive spots in TV advertising.

What did the advertising campaigns cost? Table 4 contains information on total advertising expenditures, but Table 9 gives a more accurate picture of the cost of specific spots. The official cost of a thirty-second advertising spot can vary enormously according to audience size, the extent of the buy, and the discount applied. For example, a thirty-second spot in overnight programming on CFTO can be as low as $50 for a local broadcast area and as high as $20,000 in a prime-time show, such as *Seinfeld*, shown nationally. Table 6 shows the range of costs relevant to the programming where election ads appeared. There is clearly a relationship between cost and election advertising, for the programming where ads are most likely to appear is generally at the lower end of the cost scale. While these are official costs, they may be significantly reduced by bulk buying or by the specific arrangements a media buyer may have formed with the station. Unfortunately, this kind of information is closely guarded

		Table 11		
	1995 Ontario Election: Estimated Audience Sizes for Party Ads on CFTO			
Date	Lib	NDP	PC	Total
05/17	1,539,000	2,349,000	1,518,000	5,406,000
05/18	314,000	60,000	353,000	727,000
05/19	1,129,000	1,038,582	994,582	3,162,164
05/20	891,164	496,000	444,000	1,831,164
05/21	358,000	430,000	327,000	1,115,000
05/22	1,280,000	815,000	771,000	2,866,000
05/23	665,000	0	413,000	1,078,000
05/24	1,015,000	2,219,000	595,000	3,829,000
05/25	187,000	1,580,000	595,000	2,362,000
05/26	60,000	869,000	945,000	1,874,000
05/27	0	1,152,000	0	1,152,000
05/28	759,164	0	0	759,164
05/29	1,144,000	1,240,000	595,000	2,979,000
05/30	1,144,000	1,889,000	418,000	3,451,000
05/31	732,000	2,026,746	1,890,582	4,649,328
06/01	247,000	1,425,000	1,656,000	3,328,000
06/02	537,000	1,295,000	1,132,000	2,964,000
06/03	210,000	1,095,000	0	1,305,000
06/04	31,000	0	327,000	358,000
06/05	1,498,000	461,000	951,000	2,910,000
06/06	939,000	397,000	1,535,000	2,871,000
Total	14679328	20837328	15460164	50976820

by political parties and the buying agents who work for them. Parties are not required to report the buying details of the ad campaign in their filings with the Commission on Election Finances, so much of the information on media buying that may be relevant to establishing fair election expenses is not available for public scrutiny.

How many viewers saw the ads? Table 11 shows the numbers of viewers who are estimated, based on BBM reports of audience sizes, to have seen specific programming containing election ads. The power of television advertising becomes apparent as soon as total numbers of viewers are calculated. According to the BBM estimates, the ads of all three parties would have been viewed almost 51 million times on one station in one area. Even though not all viewers would have been eligible to vote, this figure represents an astounding level of coverage for the GTA electorate by only one of many stations in the area. The appeal of television advertising for political campaigns is evident in figures that suggest viewers can be reached directly many times during the election. No other medium can reach audiences of such size or provide such repeated exposure.

How effective were the ad campaigns? As I mentioned at the beginning of the chapter, establishing the effectiveness of ad campaigns by observing their effects on voters is almost an impossibly complex problem. Voting decisions are a mixture of expressible and underlying reactions to political ideas and personalities. But in spite of these obstacles, there is sufficient evidence to venture some conclusions on the importance of the ad campaigns to the outcome of the 1995 election.

Strategists of every party acknowledged the disciplined and focused Conservative campaign, which managed not only to pick the issues that were most disturbing to the electorate, but also to sell solutions that were credible and that the Tories could be trusted to carry out. The ad campaign reflected this long-term planning and discipline and laid the groundwork for the growth in support that carried the Conservatives into office. As Leslie Noble put it:

Our ads were extremely effective: they were simple and to the point, there weren't a whole bunch of them. The worst thing you can do in advertising is to mix your message, repetition is everything. Really, we only had four ads, the Liberals had ten or twelve ads, several of them running. When we look at the postwrit studies that we've done, people knew exactly what our message was. They had no idea what the Liberal messages were … 70 per cent of the people said they couldn't identify a Liberal policy or a Liberal message from that campaign. I think advertising played a very big role …[20]

Tom Long, the Conservative campaign chair, underlined Noble's comments in saying:

The overall strategy was to keep it simple and to drive the points home and to dominate the media agenda and the issues agenda. The advertising simply fed into that. We wanted to be aggressively comparative with the Liberals so that people understood the difference between the two options. We always believed that Bob Rae was irrelevant to the process.[21]

The Conservative ad campaign was further boosted by the spot advantage it held over the other two parties. Not only did the Tories dominate the spot battle on a number of stations but their buy was timed to provide plenty of response or attack possibilities at the end of the campaign. But it is still impossible to establish any causal relationship between a good ad campaign and an election victory. The Tories could have been dreadfully wrong. They certainly were in 1990, when their equally hard-hitting and focused ads gained them virtually no return. But that was in the context of some forceful NDP ads that seemed to catch the mood of frustration in the electorate in the same way the Tory ads did in 1995. That the winning party always has the best campaign advertising is probably more an unreflective saying than the truth.

Advertising by the Conservatives has to be seen in the context of the two very ill focused and badly managed advertising campaigns that ran in opposition to them. On the other hand, whether anything more successful could have been achieved by either the Liberal or the NDP campaign is open to question. Both campaigns lacked a clear message and were hobbled by decisions to have those messages conveyed by unpopular or unknown leaders. Their attempts to establish the credibility of their message through the leader were similarly doomed to failure. Inasmuch as the Conservative polling picked up these weaknesses, the NDP and the Liberals also should have seen them. The decision to place Bob Rae at the head of the campaign did nothing to win back alienated NDP supporters or gain new votes. And despite attempts to make Lyn McLeod seem like a leader, the Liberals' ads only played into the hard-edged Conservative campaign, which made her seem vacillating in comparison.

If there is a lesson, it may be the obvious one: poorly managed ad campaigns usually reflect poorly managed campaigns that usually result in election losses. At least that much is true in the case of the 1995 Ontario election.

What do the ads tell us about the party strategies? None of the ads from the 1995 Ontario campaign are likely to make the highlight reels of great political advertising. They were mostly low-budget, unimaginative creations that followed well-established techniques and story lines. The Tories' "Weathervane" ad and stark compare-

and-contrast ads and the Liberals' tightrope walker all have long histories in American campaign advertising.

The NDP Ads

The first wave of NDP ads, "Social Contract, Add Up, Taxes, 54%, and Health," were strangely targeted, low-budget spots that featured Bob Rae, the sitting premier and leader of the Ontario NDP or "printed stills" (i.e., a printed message comparing party policies, with no moving visual images) with a voice-over. "Social Contract," "Taxes," and "Health" featured Rae shot on what appears to be the same set, the interior of a house, and standing in front of a multipaned window with a sunny view outside, although the light is dim because of an awning, the time of day, or the orientation of the window. Rae is dressed in a dark business suit with tie and is shot from the chest or shoulders up. His image fills more than one-third of the screen, in an unusually powerful representation. The home setting and the size of the head and shoulders must surely have been intended to create a degree of intimacy, the feeling of someone talking to viewers in their own living rooms. But the effect is the opposite. The size of the representation verges on the aggressive. Rae's image was never one of the folksy politician, at ease with voters and able to talk with them. Rather, an intellectual aloofness seemed a staple of his public image. The suit and tie appear to negate the desired familiarity and the erratic hand movements used to punctuate his words make him seem ill at ease. The remaining two ads of the first wave, "Add Up" and "54%," show white lettering on a black background, and a female voice reads the words. Both are fifteen-second ads.

The logic and argument of the NDP ads are as questionable as the visual content. The ads have a defensive tone and at the same time an attacking line of argument. With the exception of the Social Contract, which is dealt with in a very defensive manner, the successes of the NDP government go unheralded. Neither did the party offer any new initiatives or proposals, instead sticking to promises of defending health care and broader Ontario interests. For the most part, the ads attack as unrealistic the promises made by the Conservatives and the Liberals. If nothing else, this approach tended to emphasize the thinness of the NDP platform, which itself seemed to have succumbed to the widely held view that the party was on the way out of office. In "Add Up" and "Taxes," the argument attacks the opposition parties for promising tax cuts while vowing to balance the budget and preserve health care spending. These promises, the ads say, "do not add up." While this may be true, the viewer is forced to choose between the credibility of an unpopular premier and that of an untried candidate in waiting. Rae's own record of broken promises did not contribute to his claims. "Health" and "54%" attack the McLeod Liberals through their association with the federal party. The argument is that the federal Liberals have loaded an unfair proportion of spending cuts onto Ontario and that they are planning further cuts to health care. One ad ("54%") ends by saying: "Lyn McLeod says [the federal budget] is a good budget. Does she really represent us?" It is understandable that the early NDP ads should target the Liberals, who were leading the polls in the first days of the campaign, but the logic of attacking the very popular federal Liberal party was misguided. Not only did Ontario voters return every federal Liberal candidate save one, but the Chrétien Liberal government still had exceptionally high approval ratings almost two years after its election.

Unlike the Conservatives and Liberals, the NDP did not prepare a campaign platform, and its promises, to the extent that they existed, were not nearly as well known as the Liberal Red Book and the Common Sense Revolution. The NDP seemed to have chosen to run on the inadequacy of its opponents' promises and on the claim that it could be trusted to do what was right and fair. As the election showed, voters had long ago rejected such claims, and in the absence of campaign material that might have turned their attention to new promises or NDP successes, they voted with their feelings and sent Bob Rae out the door.

The decision to make Rae the focus of the early NDP ads, to attack the opposition parties from the outset, and to offer little in the way of promises or platform was a poor strategy. Within the NDP, Rae was seen as a leader who had refused to follow many of the party's basic principles and who strongly believed that the NDP had to moderate its left-leaning policies if it was to remain in government. His strategy alienated the left wing of the party over such issues as the failure to bring in the promised public auto insurance plan and angered labour supporters by reopening collective-bargaining contracts to implement the job-saving Social Contract. To make Rae the focus of the ads only served to remind supporters of his alleged heresies. Liberal and Conservative supporters who occasionally gave the premier grudging support during his time in office were never likely to support him during the election so long as there were opposition parties that were willing to advocate a business agenda.

The focus on Rae was never likely to convince them to vote for the NDP. Attacking the opposition parties only emphasized the absence of NDP promises. Voters were never told what the NDP would do if returned to office. The appeal was based solely on a call to trust the government to do what was fair and right. In the end, this appeal depended on credibility, and given the NDP's string of broken promises while in office, it was truly a no-win strategy to get into a contest of credibility with opposition parties that could not be shown to have broken a promise.

Conservative Ads

The Conservative ads differed greatly from those of the other two parties. While Harris was the focus of the Conservative ads, just as Mcleod and Rae were for their parties' spots, the Conservative promises were clearly and simply presented, and the representations of Harris were invariably of a person "on the move," someone who was going to get things done. This image of the leader in action was missing from both Liberal and NDP spots, which tended to present their leaders in static shots.

The Conservative ads of the first week were "Welfare/Quotas," "Taxes," and "Vision," the last receiving by far the least air time in the early weeks. "Welfare/Quotas" and "Taxes" were stark compare-and-contrast ads composed entirely of stills with narration. The Harris party policies were contrasted to the McLeod party policies, the Tories' party policies in blue and the Liberals' in red. The ads targeted the Liberal policies as the main threat and focused on three issues: putting welfare recipients to work, cutting taxes to produce jobs, and removing the NDP's employment equity legislation, which the Tories characterized as unfair job quotas, a damaging tag the NDP ads never tried to contest. For example, on workfare, the text and narration read: "Mike Harris will require welfare recipients to work for benefits. Lyn McLeod opposes work for welfare. You will not hear Lyn McLeod talking about mandatory workfare." The ads were very simple in text and visuals and focused tightly on the three issues that the Conservative polling had identified as winning issues. Putting Harris above the party, which was seldom mentioned, served to avoid the embarrassing connection with the highly unpopular federal Conservative government of Brian Mulroney, which had been soundly defeated in 1993. It also helped the Harris Tories appeal to federal Reform Party supporters, who were much more at home with Harris policies than they might have been with traditionally centrist Ontario PC policies. Focusing on Lyn McLeod was equally effective because it separated the Ontario Liberal party from the popular federal Liberals of Jean Chrétien. Moreover, McLeod was an unknown quantity about to contest her first and last election as leader of the Ontario Liberals. It was fairly safe to assume that voters would not know where McLeod stood on these issues and so were unlikely to be able to disagree with the Tory version of her policies. All three ads in the first wave — "Welfare/Quotas," "Taxes," and "Vision" — ended with stills of Harris and some version of the campaign theme "Common Sense for a Change."

"Vision" was very different from the other two spots. It was a busy ad, including some fifteen different shots of Harris with all sorts of citizens: the elderly, young mothers, workers, students, members of different cultural communities, northerners, the press, and so on. The shots, from the opening frame of two Harris campaign buses to the final logo, moved at a fast pace, giving the impression of a young, vigorous, casual, approachable leader who is consulting with citizens and ready to do things. Harris was pictured in shirtsleeves, at ease with and close to the other people in the shots. There was a feeling of intimacy, of a candidate who understands the values of different communities. This contrasted markedly with the Liberal and NDP ads, which were stuffy and lacking in intimacy or any shots that showed the candidate in close contact with voters. Overlaid on these images was text highlighting the three Conservative campaign issues: end unfair job quotas, cut taxes to create jobs, and make people work for welfare. "Vision" followed an established spot format that has a long history. In that sense it was not creative in any way; yet in contrast to the opposition ads, it had a feeling of energy and promise that other ads lacked. Not only did this ad promise common-sense change, but the visuals appeared to illustrate it as well. There was a feeling of moving forward that began with the image of the campaign bus and was carried through the quick succession of images that showed Harris in motion, descending from an airplane and meeting people in various settings. In contrast to the staged and motionless images of the NDP and Liberal ads, "Vision" had a compelling image of forward motion that captured the antidote for the prevailing mood of slipping backwards, of opportunities at a standstill, of prolonged economic downturn. But one can make too much of this ad. It was far from unique; the Peterson Liberals ran very similar ads in the 1990 campaign, and the genre is a staple of campaign advertising. More significant is the failure of the other two parties to produce anything containing a similar level of energy. While the NDP ads of 1990 had correctly mirrored the sense of frustration at that time, these spots completely missed the prevailing mood of "wanting to move on" that may have been present in 1995.

It is easy to praise the ads of the winning party, as ad creators are likely to do. In this case it was not the originality or creativity of the Conservative ads, but rather the contrast between them and the ads of the other parties that worked to the party's advantage.

Liberal Ads

The Liberal ads of the first week concentrated entirely on the Liberal plan, or Red Book, as it became known. The two ads, "Action Plan" and "Experts/Balanced Budget," were largely stills of the action plan itself and endorsements of the plan by notables. Lyn McLeod appeared very briefly at the end of the second ad, addressing the camera from chest up while sitting in a large leather upholstered chair that generated an image of wealth, power, and authority.

"Action Plan" is an unusual ad in that it consists entirely of changing stills of different pages of the Liberal campaign manifesto. Without doubt, this makes for dull visuals: showing a book defeats the purpose of both print and television. As one observer has noted, "Television is a visual medium. The viewer must be *shown*, not told."[22] On the other hand, the ad reveals something about the Liberal campaign strategy: strategists must have concluded that what voters wanted most was assurance that the next government had a plan and was prepared to implement it. This strategy must have partly followed from the federal Liberals' success with their Red Book in 1993. The ads mentioned specific promises to balance the budget and protect health care as ways to a stronger economy. The argument underlying both ads was that governments should have a plan, that the Liberals had a good one endorsed by people who should be able to judge its merit, and that, therefore, the voters should choose the Liberals over the other two parties. As political discourse, this was rather thin gruel, thinner than the Tories' specific policy statements, though a slight improvement over the NDP's no-promises campaign. It contrasted unfavourably with the Tories' ads, which offered promises on specific policies. The Liberals, with a new leader and a hazy policy position in the centre, only seemed to exacerbate the uncertainty surrounding their policies.

Unlike the other two parties, the Liberals used endorsements by several notables to lend credibility to their platform. While the experts called the plan achievable, none had names that would be recognized by even a tiny percentage of voters. Since endorsements work best when the audience is familiar with the figure recommending the policy, the person, or the product, this Liberal strategy must have had very little effect.

The Liberal ads that appeared late in the campaign were equally unfocused, "Tightrope" perhaps being the best example. The ad featured a dimly lit, carnival-like figure shown from the waist down walking a tightrope with a balancing pole. The relevance of the image was far from obvious other than the fact that the Tories were promising something that was risky. In fact, the Tory promises of tax cuts and reduced spending through welfare reform seemed, if only superficially, to balance out.

Conclusions

Despite the fact that television advertising is arguably the most important part of election campaigns, systematic knowledge of aspects of campaign advertising is still rather limited. This chapter has begun to address this lack of knowledge. While it has not directly answered still-intriguing questions about the effect that ads have on individual voters, it has begun to fill in important information about the basics of campaign advertising. Those basics now include information about media buying strategies and their importance to campaign success. The extent to which the Conservatives outdistanced the other two parties in the size and timing of their media buy raises some questions about regulating campaign television advertising to ensure fairness while allowing the parties room to pursue strategies that best fit their potential electorate. The chapter also provided some detail about the programming during which campaign ads appear. There were some important differences between parties in the choice of programming, though obviously the availability of spots and the speed with which the parties entered the market affected the kinds of spots they were able to obtain. This chapter also illustrated how the parties are limited to placing ads in relatively inexpensive programming, and how expensive some advertising spots can be. With advertising costs forming such a large part of overall campaign expenses, the high cost of spots drives the need to raise ever-larger sums of money to pay for campaigns, thus placing upward pressure on campaign expenditure limits. Raising money for campaigns is a time-consuming organizational task that some may argue comes to dominate other important functions of political parties. At what point do political organizations dedicate too much of their resources to raising funds and plotting ad campaigns and not enough to the development of ideas for governing? As citizens, should we be thinking about ways to restrict these expenditures through free television time or a limit on the number of spots, thereby lowering the costs of entry for political parties and perhaps allowing the discussion of policies to rise above the discussion of politics in the dialect of advertising?

The interviews with campaign strategists quoted in this chapter demonstrate that campaigns are directed by small groups of people who design the content and tone of a party's message. When strategists' patterns of thinking are dominated by the language and ideas of advertising, of manipulation, of image creation, and of issue and slogan selection, there is less room for discussions in the more traditional political language of common causes and social justice. Advertising is about persuading people to do the things that are to the advantage of advertisers. Democratic politics should be about making it possible for people to do the things that they believe to be important. Advertising is not primarily about truth-telling. When pressed, all consumers recognize that a product will seldom live up to the fantastic claims that are often made about it. As citizens, we should not wish to encourage the making of the same kind of unbelievable claims about our future, for that will only breed cynicism about the ability of democratic politics to produce solutions.

Finally, the 1995 Ontario election has proven to be one of the most significant in the province's history, making the much-talked-of win in 1990 by the NDP seem rather staid by comparison. The Harris government has set in motion radical changes in the relationship between citizens and their governments. Our expectations of what we must provide for ourselves, and what the state will provide, have undergone serious rewriting. Whether voters imagined that this might be the result of electing a Conservative government is an open question. That they took the plunge and voted the Tories into office is partly due to a brilliantly conceived and executed advertising campaign. The Conservatives did not win the election of 1995 because of their ads or media buying, but the discipline they brought to the campaign and the forethought they gave to their advertising campaign laid the groundwork for their victory.

Endnotes

1. The research conducted for this chapter was supported by a grant from the Social Sciences and Humanities Research Council of Canada. The grant holders are Fred Fletcher, Edouard Cloutier, Denis Moniere, David Taras, and me. I would like to thank Gene Costain, Todd Harris, and Joanne McLellan for assisting with various research tasks and Fred Fletcher for advice and comments on a draft of the chapter.

2. See, for example: Harold Clarke, Jane Jenson, Lawrence LeDuc, and Jon Pammett, *Absent Mandate: Interpreting Change in Canadian Elections*, 2nd ed., Toronto: Gage, 1991; Alan Frizzell, Jon Pammett, and Anthony Westell, *The Canadian General Election of 1988*, Ottawa: Carleton University Press, 1989; Richard Johnston et al., *Letting the People Decide: Dynamics of a Canadian Election*, Montreal and Kingston: McGill-Queen's University Press, 1992; Jean Créte, "Television, Advertising and Canadian Elections," in Fred Fletcher, ed., *Media and Voters in Canadian Election Campaigns*, volume 18 of the Royal Commission on Electoral Reform and Party Financing, Toronto: Dundurn Press, 1991; Stephen Kline and William Leiss, "Political Broadcast Advertising," in Fred Fletcher, ed., *Election Broadcasting in Canada*, volume 21 of the research studies of the Royal Commission on Electoral Reform and Party Financing; Walter I. Romanow, Walter C. Soderlund, and Richard Price, "Negative Political Advertising. An Analysis of Research Findings in Light of Canadian Practice," in Janet Hiebert, ed., *Political Ethics: A Canadian Perspective*, volume 12 of the research studies of the Royal Commission on Electoral Reform and Party Financing. For an insider account see Gerald Caplan, Michael Kirby, and Hugh Segal, *Election: The Issues, the Strategies, the Aftermath,* Toronto: Prentice-Hall, 1989.

3. Not to say that there have not been attempts to answer this question. For examples, see: Stephen Ansolabehere and Shanto Iyengar, *Going Negative: How Attack Ads Shrink and Polarize the Electorate*, New York: Free Press, 1995; M. Basil, C. Schooler, and B. Reeves, "Positive and Negative Political Advertising: Effectiveness of Ads and Perceptions of Candidates," in F. Bioccaa, ed., *Television and Political Advertising: Vol. 1. Psychological Processes*, Hillsdale, NJ: Lawrence Erlbaum, 1991; Robert G. Meadow and Lee Sigelman, "Some Effects and Non-effects of Campaign Commercials," *Political Behaviour* 4. (1982): 163–175.

4. The following stations were included in the sample:
CFPL	London	Independent
CFTO	Toronto	CTV affiliate
CHBX	Sault Ste. Marie	CTV affiliate
CHCH	Hamilton	Independent Westcom
CHEX	Peterborough	CBC affiliate
CHNB	North Bay	CBC affiliate
CITY	Toronto	Independent
CKCO	Kitchener	CTV affiliate

CKPR	Thunder Bay	CBC affiliate
CKVR	Barrie	CBC affiliate
CKWS	Kingston	CBC affiliate

Bowden's Media Directory, Bowden/Information Service, Toronto, June 1994 lists thirty Ontario stations. Some stations, such as TVO and La Chaîne Française, TVO's French-language channel, do not take ads. I am grateful to the CRTC and especially to Rob McLeod for allowing access to these data.

5. I am grateful to Gene Costain for completing and transcribing many of these interviews.

6. This includes research on American campaign advertising and political advertising in other nations. It may be that this type of analysis is impossible due to the lack of station logs maintained by the regulator, the CRTC.

7. David Lindsey, principal secretary to Mike Harris (interview), August 18, 1995.

8. Interview conducted on August 18, 1995.

9. Jim McLean, senior media adviser to Lyn McLeod (interview), August 23, 1995.

10. Interview conducted on August 18, 1995.

11. Interview conducted on August 25 1995.

12. Dennis Young (interview), September 25, 1995.

13. Jim McLean, senior media adviser to Lyn McLeod (interview), August 23, 1995.

14. Rosemary Barr (interview), September 18, 1995

15. Bob Richardson (interview), November 1, 1995

16. Michael Marzolini (interview), October 27, 1995.

17. Michael Marzolini (interview), October 27, 1995

18. The 1990 NDP Ontario election ads were almost entirely in the form of simulated news reports.

19. I would like to thank CFTO's Jeff Dyke and Mark Kahansky for this information.

20. Interview conducted on August 18, 1995.

21. Interview conducted on August 11, 1995.

22. Dorothy D. Nesbit, *Videostyle in Senate Campaigns*, Knoxville: University of Tennessee Press, 1988, 43.

6

Changing Patterns of Party Support in Ontario

Geoffrey E. Hale

This chapter analyzes changing patterns of voter support and party loyalty in Ontario. It does this by combining riding-level Canada Census data from 1981 and 1991 and riding-by-riding outcomes from the five Ontario general elections held between 1981 and 1995. It also examines the effects of incumbency and the relationship between socioeconomic factors and election results in different geographic regions of the province.

At 44.9 per cent, the Harris Conservatives' share of the popular vote was marginally higher than the shares won by Bill Davis in 1971 and 1981. The composition of the PC vote in 1995 was also different. Compared with PC governments of the Davis era, the Harris Conservatives made significant gains in the rural and urban ridings of southwestern Ontario and in the Hamilton-Niagara region — both in the number of seats won and in the share of the popular vote (see

Seats/	1995		1990		1987		1985		1981	
votes	#	%	#	%	#	%	#	%	#	%
PC	82	44.9	20	23.5	16	24.7	52	37.0	70	44.8
Lib	30	31.1	36	32.4	95	47.2	48	37.9	34	32.7
NDP	17	20.5	74	37.6	19	25.8	25	23.8	21	20.6
Other	1	3.5	0	6.6	0	2.3	0	1.3	0	0.9

Table 12
Ontario Election Results: 1981-95

	Table 13 Distribution of Conservative Seats/Votes						
			Average		Average		
	Total PC 1995		PC Majority		PC Minority		
	Seats		(1971 1981)		(1975 1977 1985)		
Seats/Votes		N	%	N	%	N	%
Central Ontario	6	6	60.5	5.5	48.9	5.0	42.7
GTA (excl. Metro)	17	17	56.4	8.5	53.7	7.7	41.3
Suburban Metro	17	10	53.2	9.0	46.6	6.0	36.1
Rural/s. town E. Ontario	11	9	50.2	11.5	48.9	9.3	46.0
Rural/s. town S.W. Ontario	14	11	46.9	8.0	43.2	5.3	36.9
Urban S.W. Ontario	14	10	41.1	5.0	35.9	2.0	31.2
Urban E. Ontario	11	4	41.0	5.5	45.0	4.0	37.3
Hamilton-Niagara	12	8	40.2	5.0	38.5	2.3	31.2
Inner Metro	13	6	34.5	8.0	43.7	5.3	35.3
N. Ontario	15	1	30.2	8.0	42.6	6.0	39.5
Total	130	82	44.9	74	44.7	53.7	38.2

Table 13). Many of the new seats that were won in 1995 had been Liberal strongholds for at least one and often two generations.

The 1995 Election — A Summary of the Results

The Progressive Conservatives

The new PC government was elected mainly on the basis of its strong support in small-town and suburban areas. It swept all seventeen fringe urban ridings in the four-county Greater Toronto Area (GTA), and all but four of the twenty-eight predominantly small-town and rural ridings in southern Ontario.

The PCs also recovered most of the seats in the suburban Toronto boroughs and in small-town eastern Ontario, seats which they had held during Davis's fourteen years as premier. The total PC vote almost doubled between 1990 and 1995, with the largest percentage gains being recorded in the suburban Toronto boroughs and the cities of southwestern Ontario. These gains more than offset the PCs' failure to recover their traditional level of support in the City of Toronto and in Northern Ontario.

The Liberals

While the PCs won the election, it is also true that the Liberals lost it. Many of the traditionally Liberal areas that had shifted to the NDP in 1990 did not return to the Liberal fold but instead shifted to the PCs. Only Essex County, the Ottawa Valley, parts of Metro Toronto, and Northern Ontario resisted the Tory tide.

Many Liberals had viewed the election results of 1990, which saw them lose control of both the major cities and rural areas of southwestern Ontario to the NDP, as an electoral fluke that would soon be remedied. Under the leadership of Robert Nixon (1967–76) and Stuart Smith (1976–82), Liberal support had been concentrated in southwestern Ontario. David Peterson (1982–90) succeeded in making the Liberals an urban party that was electorally competitive in the fast-growing areas in and around Toronto, Ottawa, and other large cities. Like its federal counterpart, the party also enjoyed strong support among recent immigrants and franco-Ontarians, and within multicultural communities. The selection of Lyn McLeod to replace Peterson in 1991 was intended to cement these bases of support while building on Liberal gains since the 1970s in Northern Ontario.

While provincewide Liberal support declined slightly from 1990, the Liberals held or increased their base of seats in urban eastern Ontario (see Table 14; six seats: 40 per cent of the popular vote), especially around Ottawa, Northern Ontario (six seats: 37 per cent), and the suburban Toronto boroughs (seven seats: 27 per cent), due largely to a sharp drop in NDP support. While between 1975 and 1985 the Liberals won slightly more than half of their seats in rural or small-town ridings, two-thirds of Liberals elected in 1990 (twenty-four of thirty-six candidates) and 1995 (twenty of thirty candidates) came from major urban or suburban areas with populations over 100,000.

The areas of strongest Liberal support in 1995 were those with the largest immigrant and French-speaking populations. The Liberals won nine of eighteen ridings with an immigrant population over 40 per cent, most of them in Metro Toronto. Six of the eleven ridings with French-speaking populations over 20 per cent (compared with a provincial average of 4.7 per cent) elected Liberals; most of the rest re-elected NDP incumbents.

The New Democrats

The New Democrats suffered their worst electoral finish, with seventeen seats, since 1963 (see Table 12). NDP support in the popular

Table 14 Distribution of Liberal Seats/Votes by Region: 1975-95								
	1995		1990		1987		1975-85	
Seats/Votes	N	%	N	%	N	%	N	%
Urban E. Ontario	6	40.5	6	41.5	9	50.3	1.5	33.2
N. Ontario	6	36.7	4	34.4	7	39.1	1.5	22.7
Rural/s. town E. Ontario	3	32.7	5	33.3	8	50.1	4.5	39.0
Hamilton-Niagara	2	32.7	1	28.7	8	45.8	5.5	37.4
Inner Metro	2	31.8	3	34.1	10	43.2	1.3	27.9
GTA (excl. Metro)	0	28.1	8	33.0	12	48.0	1.3	30.0
Rural/s. town S.W. Ontario	2	27.1	3	30.3	13	50.6	10.3	46.7
Suburban Metro	7	27.0	6	34.2	14	49.2	2.5	29.1
Urban S.W. Ontario	2	26.9	0	29.2	11	49.9	8.8	43.0
Central Ontario	0	21.1	0	26.1	3	39.5	1.0	33.0
Total	30	31.1	36	32.4	95	47.2	38	34.9

vote, at 20.5 per cent, was below its worst previous showing since the 1950s (in 1981). The NDP's surviving MPPs are clustered in Northern Ontario and in lower-income neighbourhoods of Toronto, London, and Hamilton. The NDP held on to most of its core vote in Metro Toronto, urban southwestern Ontario, and most of Northern Ontario. However, only ten of the fifty-six first-time New Democrat MPPs elected in 1990 succeeded in winning re-election — most of them from traditionally NDP seats.

This is attributable in part to voter frustration over the state of the economy and to the decision of many union activists to abandon the party in 1995 in a reaction to the NDP's Social Contract legislation, which imposed wage reductions on many public sector employees. The NDP found it increasingly difficult to reconcile the interests of its traditional supporters among industrial workers, whose living standards declined sharply during the recession, with those of government employees, who had benefited from the rapid growth in government spending and taxation during the late 1980s and the NDP's early years in power. This created an environment in which many traditional Liberal and NDP supporters became increasingly open to Conservative arguments that blamed the spiralling deficit on excessive government spending, as well as on the fiscal effects of the recession.

Minor Parties

The effect of minor parties on electoral outcomes was not as signifi- cant in 1995 as in 1990, when independent and minor party candi- dates won 6.6 per cent of the vote. The Conservatives succeeded in positioning themselves as the party of social conservatism in 1995 — in sharp contrast to the socially liberal, urban-oriented Toryism of the Davis years — and appear to have reclaimed much of the culturally alienated small-town electorate that gave both the Family Coalition and the Confederation of Regions parties sizable votes in more than thirty ridings in 1990 and catapulted the Reform Party to second place in the popular vote in the 1993 federal election.

The most successful minor party in 1995, as in 1990, was the traditionalist, pro-life Family Coalition Party: ten of its fifty-three candidates won more than 5 per cent of the vote. The Natural Law Party ran the largest number of candidates — sixty-nine. Former NDP MPP Peter North, running for re-election in Elgin riding, bene- fited from a split in the local Conservative organization to become the first independent candidate elected to the legislature in Ontario since 1934.

The Decline of Incumbency

The 1995 election continues a pattern of electoral volatility that can best be seen in the declining power of incumbency in Ontario politics (see Table 16). Elections since 1985 have seen a sharp drop in the re-election rate of incumbents from 81.2 per cent in 1985 to 58.4 per cent in 1990 and 44.8 per cent in 1995, and an even higher rate of turnover in open seats. Newly elected candidates account for 73 of the 130 MPs (56.1 per cent) in the current legislature.

By contrast, 89.8 per cent of incumbents seeking re-election were successful in the four provincial elections between 1971 and 1981. Most party turnover took place in open seats not contested by an incumbent — particularly in the 1975 election, in which the Conser- vatives were reduced to minority government status. Table 16 sum- marizes the declining effect of incumbency in provincial elections and the overall growth of electoral volatility since the mid-1970s.

A major factor in the realignment of rural ridings was the defeat or retirement of a majority of the incumbent MPPs from rural and small-town ridings in southern Ontario in or after the 1990 election.

Table 15 Distribution of NDP Seats/Votes by Region: 1975-95								
	1995		1990		1981-87		1975-77	
					Average		Average	
	N	%	N	%	N	%	N	%
N. Ontario	8	31.6	10	42.1	6.0	34.6	7.5	39.5
Inner Metro	5	31.6	10	44.0	5.0	30.7	8.0	35.3
Urban S.W. Ontario	2	26.9	12	45.8	1.3	26.9	4.0	29.1
Hamilton-Niagara	2	23.9	11	48.9	3.7	29.8	4.5	32.8
Suburban Metro	0	20.9	8	38.5	3.3	25.6	6.0	31.1
Rural/ s. town S.W. Ontario	0	17.8	8	35.1	0.3	15.2	0	15.1
Central Ontario	0	16.0	3	33.7	0	19.0	0	26.3
Urban E. Ontario	0	15.6	3	29.5	1.0	22.2	3.5	31.6
GTA (excl. Metro)	10	13.4	5	30.1	1.0	19.7	2.0	29.6
Rural/ s. town E. Ontario	0	13.3	4	28.1	0	12.2	0	16.9
Total	17	20.5	74	37.6	21.6	24.1	35.5	28.6

These ridings were the backbone of the old Liberal party caucus between 1965 and 1990. Before 1987, rural Ontario voters tended to re-elect about 90 per cent of incumbent MPPs, regardless of party affiliation. Party turnover was much more likely to take place in open seats.

The weakening of traditional party affiliations in rural areas resulted in part from the transformation of the Liberals into a primarily urban party, the growth of the minor party vote as an expression of rural alienation from the political system, and the freakish election of fifteen New Democrats in rural ridings in 1990. It remains to be seen whether the wave of Conservative backbenchers elected in predominantly rural ridings in 1995 can consolidate their positions into a pattern of long-term incumbency similar to that enjoyed by their predecessors of the 1960s and 1970s.

Three Party Competition and Election Results

While Ontario is a functioning three-party system in that the Liberals, Conservatives, and New Democrats regularly form sizable contingents in the legislature and obtain more than 20 per cent of the popular vote, effective three-party competition is the norm in rela-

Table 16 Patterns of Incumbency and Party Turnover in Ontario Elections: 1971-95				
	Toronto/GTA	Other Cities Over 100,000	Rural/ small-town	Total
Incumbent Re-elected	(%)	(%)	(%)	(%)
1971	79.3	88.0	92.3	87.1
1975	80.0	80.8	82.5	81.3
1977	94.6	87.1	95.5	92.9
1981	88.6	79.4	92.1	86.9
1985	71.4	83.3	89.1	81.2
1987	71.0	69.4	81.2	73.3
1990	54.8	45.9	59.4	58.4
1995	40.5	36.6	60.6	44.8
1971-81 Average	86.5	83.6	90.7	89.8
1985-95 Average	62.3	56.9	73.3	62.3
Overall Average	71.0	68.8	82.7	74.5
Same Party Returned (Open Seat)				
1971	60.0	55.6	90.0	70.8
1975	50.0	33.3	42.9	42.3
1977	33.3	83.3	100.0	76.9
1981	40.0	66.7	100.0	63.6
1985	66.7	72.7	57.1	66.7
1990	80.0	16.7	37.5	42.1
1995	20.0	50.0	33.3	30.8
1971-81 Average	47.8	55.6	79.2	60.8
1985-95 Average	48.4	44.0	35.7	42.9
Overall Average	48.1	50.0	55.8	51.3

tively few ridings. For the purposes of this study, effective three-party competition is defined as occurring in those ridings in which the vote for the two unsuccessful major parties is at least half that of the winning party.

In 1995, effective three-party competition existed in thirty-five constituencies (see Table 17). A review of election results between 1981 and 1995 suggests that, with the exception of the election in

	1995				1990				Both
Table 17 **Outcomes in Three-Party Contests by Region (1990, 1995)**									
	PC	Lib	NDP	Total	PC	Lib	NDP	Total	
Metro Toronto	6	0	3	(9)	1	5	4	(10)	3
GTA	0	0	0	(0)	1	9	4	(14)	0
Hamilton-Niagara	5	0	1	(6)	3	0	0	(3)	0
S.W. Ontario									
Urban	6	0	1	(7)	2	0	3	(5)	3
Rural/small-town	4	0	1	(5)	3	2	7	(12)	4
E. Ontario									
Urban	0	2	0	(2)	1	3	2	(6)	1
Rural/small town	1	0	0	(1)	1	2	3	(6)	1
Central Ontario	0	0	0	(0)	1	0	3	(4)	0
N. Ontario	0	1	4	(5)	0	0	0	(0)	0
Total	22	3	10	(35)	13	22	26	(61)	12

1990, effective three-party competition is a significant and ongoing factor in fewer than thirty constituencies — about two-thirds of which could be described as swing ridings in which all three parties are reasonably competitive (see Table 18).

Between 25 and 35 per cent of ridings could be defined as "safe seats" — those held consistently by one party for at least four elections or in at least six of the last eight elections. (By this definition, the number of safe seats dropped by about 20 per cent in the 1995 election; see Table 19.) Since identifying safe seats from the results of individual elections is inherently risky, given the transience of voter loyalties in recent years, one might also define a safe seat as one in which the winning candidate has majority support and no opposition candidate wins more than half the winner's votes, if only on the grounds that such margins would tend to discourage capable challengers. Winning candidates in thirty-three ridings won by such margins in 1995.

About sixty ridings could be described as two-party marginals, in the sense that the same two parties are regularly competitive and the riding has changed hands in recent years (see Table 18). Except in 1990, forty-two of the two-party marginal districts are characterized by PC-Liberal competition, about a dozen (mainly in lower- and

Table 18 Riding Level Party Competition: 1981-95					
	PC	Lib	NDP	Total	Per Cent
Safe Seats	12	9	9	30	23.1
Two-Party Marginals (4+ elections)					
Mainly Lib-PC	40	2	0	42	32.3
Mainly Lib-NDP	1	8	3	12	9.2
Mainly PC-NDP	4	1	0	5	3.8
Total					45.3
Three-Party Comp.	17	2	1	20	15.4
Stable one-party control	0	3	1	4	3.1
Mainly PC-NDP	4			4	3.1
Mainly Lib-NDP	0	2	0	2	1.5
Total					23.1

middle-income urban areas) by Liberal-NDP competition, and about five by PC-NDP competition.

Economic Factors and Voting Patterns: 1995

The effects of the severe economic restructuring and social dislocations of the early 1990s can be clearly seen when comparing the economic and income characteristics of individual ridings with riding level results:

- a majority of industrial and middle-income ridings swung to the Conservatives, away from the New Democrats, generally at levels above those won by the Davis Tories during the 1970s and 1980s;

- upper-income ridings voted heavily for the Conservatives after supporting the Liberals in 1987 and, to a lesser extent, in 1990;

- lower-income urban ridings were split between the Liberals and the New Democrats;

- the Liberals won higher levels of support in ridings with higher-than-average levels of public sector employment.

	Table 19 Safe Seats: 1971-95							
	1995 Election				Ridings Won Six or More Times by Same Party Since 1971			
	PC	L	NDP	Total	PC	L	NDP	Total
Metro Toronto								
Inner Toronto	0	0	0	(0)	4	1*	5	(10)
Suburban boroughs	2	0	0	(2)	4	1	0	(5)
GTA	9	0	0	(9)	4	0	0	(4)
Hamilton-Niagara	1	0	0	(1)	1	1	1	(3)
S.W. Ontario								
Urban	2	0	0	(2)	0	1	1	(2)
Rural/small-town	3	1	0	(4)	3	1	0	(4)
E. Ontario								
Urban	2	1	0	(3)	1	1	0	(2)
Rural/small-town	4	0	0	(4)	5	2*	0	(7)
Central Ontario	6	0	0	(6)	6	0	0	(6)
N. Ontario	1	1	0	(2)	1*	0	4	(5)
Total	30	3	0	(33)	29	7	11	(47)
Excluding 1995 election					29	12	17	(58)

*Includes ridings held for five consecutive elections: Parkdale (L),Prescott-Russell (L) and Nipissing (PC).
+Based on current riding boundaries; includes predecessor ridings from redistributions of 1975,1987.

After two generations of more or less steady economic growth and improvements in the average standard of living, Ontarians experienced severe economic dislocation and declining household incomes during the early 1990s. While there are wide variations in the economic experiences of individuals during this period, as a general rule, public sector employment increased 12 per cent between 1988 and 1994, and public sector incomes continued to increase despite the partial rollbacks of the NDP's Social Contract, while those in many parts of the private sector experienced significant declines. For example, manufacturing employment dropped 8 per cent between 1988 and 1994 (see Table 20).

Table 20 Employment in Goods–Producing Industries, Government				
	1985	1988	1992	1994
Manufacturing and construction Employment (in '000)	1,300	1,397	1,159	1,285
1985 = 100	100.0	107.4	89.2	98.8
% of total employment	28.2	27.2	23.2	24.9
Community Services (Health Education & Social Services) Employment (in '000)	640	750	831	867
1985 = 100	100.0	117.2	129.8	135.5
% of total employment	13.9	14.6	16.6	16.8
Public Administration (all levels of government) Employment (in '000)	303	315	334	326
1985 = 100	100.0	104.0	100.2	107.6
% of total employment	6.6	6.1	6.7	6.3
Source: *1995 Fiscal and Economic Statement*, Toronto; Ministry of Finance, November 1995, Table 39.				

The problems of structural economic adjustment are reflected in the wide swings since the early 1980s in party support of the province's industrial ridings (defined here as those with manufacturing employment in excess of 20 per cent of the labour force in 1991 and over 26 per cent in 1981). While the PCs failed to win a single industrial constituency in 1990, they captured twenty-five of forty-one industrial ridings in 1995, and ten of seventeen ridings with a manufacturing workforce of 25 per cent or more (see Table 21). This increase included significant gains in industrial cities such as Kitchener, Cambridge, Oshawa, Brantford, Hamilton, and Niagara Falls.

A major factor in these gains appears to have been the Tories' ability to exploit the frustration of middle-income voters about policies of high taxation and high deficits. Arguably, many of these voters, facing declining after-tax incomes since the mid-1980s, responded favourably to Tory proposals to reduce taxes and welfare rates, and to end the rationing of employment opportunities through employment equity legislation. Table 21 analyzes historical voting patterns in ridings with above-average levels of employment in manufacturing.

Ironically, to regain power at Queen's Park, the Tories have had to shed their traditional image as the "government party" and run

							PC Majority		PC Minority	
Seats/	1995		1990		1987		Elections		Elections	
votes	#	%	#	%	#	%	#	%	#	%
PC	25	40.5	0	17.8	2	19.5	16.5	38.0	10.7	32.9
Lib	8	31.8	9	30.7	29	45.7	11.0	32.0	13.3	33.3
NDP	7	24.3	32	44.7	10	32.6	8.5	29.6	15.0	32.8

Table 21
Voting Patterns in Industrial Ridings: 1971-95

against the institutions that they built during their forty-two years in office during and after World War II. This is reflected in their relatively weak performance in the twenty-seven ridings with above-average employment (25 per cent or more) in the broader public sector — direct government employment, education, health and social services (see Table 22). While the Conservatives won ten of these ridings, most of these had average incomes well over the provincial average. The Liberals ran significantly ahead of the Tories in ridings, mainly in the Ottawa area, with proportions of public sector employment over 35 per cent.

Income and Voter Choice

The Harris Conservatives regained overwhelming support from upper-income constituencies, as defined by average household income in 1991 (see Table 23). The Tories won twenty-six of twenty-nine ridings whose household incomes averaged 110 per cent or more ($57,447) of the provincial average ($52,225 in 1991). The PC vote in these twenty-nine ridings averaged 54.6 per cent in 1995 — a level comparable to support from the same areas for PC majority governments in 1971 and 1981.

The growth of (relatively affluent) suburban populations of the GTA, Ottawa-Carleton, and Hamilton-Wentworth regions, while not yet fully reflected in the redistribution of riding boundaries, has gradually worked to the Tories' advantage by increasing the number of upper-income ridings.

However, the Conservatives' largest gains were mainly in middle-income ridings, many of them traditionally the scene of three-way contests among the major parties (see Table 24). The Harris Tories won twenty-two of the forty ridings with average household incomes of 85 to 100 per cent of the provincial average — more than Bill

Table 22 — Levels of Party Support in Ridings with Public Sector Employment over 25 Per Cent (1995)				
			Over 35% of Jobs in Public Sector	
	Seats	% Vote	Seats	% Vote
PC	10	39.1	2	36.7
Lib	11	36.8	6	44.2
NDP	5	21.7	0	16.6
Other	0	2.4	0	2.5

Table 23 — Voting Patterns in Upper-Income Ridings										
(Average Household Income >110% of Ontario Average)										
								1971,1981		1975,1977,1985
Seats/	1995		1990		1987		Average		Average	
votes	#	%	#	%	#	%	#	%	#	%
PC	26	54.6	9	31.8	5	30.2	20.0	54.6	16.0	42.7
Lib	3	30.0	13	34.6	24	50.3	3.5	27.0	6.7	33.4
NDP	0	13.3	7	28.3	0	17.2	0.0	17.8	1.3	22.9
Other	0	2.2	0	5.2	0	2.2	0.0	0.5	0.0	0.5

Davis managed in his majority government elections of 1971 and 1981. The collapse of PC support in middle-income ridings, three-quarters of them urban, had been central to the Tories' third-place finishes in 1987 and 1990. In 1995, many of these ridings experienced a sharp decline in voter turnout, with many traditional NDP voters appearing to have stayed home.

Voting patterns in lower-income ridings, defined as those with average household incomes at least 15 per cent below the Ontario average, are sharply different in urban and small-town/rural ridings (see Table 25). The PCs have rarely been competitive in the majority of the lower-income urban ridings; these ridings often split their votes between the Liberals and the New Democrats. The majority of lower-income urban ridings are characterized by either single-party dominance with well-entrenched Liberal or NDP incumbents or two-way competition between the Liberals and the New Democrats. A minority of lower-income urban ridings (e.g., Brantford, Peterbor-

Table 24 Voting Patterns in Lower–Middle-Income Ridings (Average Household Income: 85-100% of Ontario Average)									
							1971, 1981		1975,1977,1985
Seats/	1995		1990		1987		Average		Average
votes	#	%	#	%	#	%	#	%	#	%
PC	22	38.9	2	18.2	3	20.5	16	39.2	10.7	33.7
Lib	10	31.0	6	29.5	24	42.6	8	30.7	8.7	31.3
NDP	8	26.6	32	46.1	13	34.7	13	29.5	19.7	33.8
Other	0	3.4	0	6.0	0	2.2	0	0.2	0.0	0.3

ough, St. Catharines-Brock) are swing ridings that have supported the winning party in at least four of the past five elections.

The Liberals won eight of the seventeen lower-income urban ridings, a gain of six from the NDP. As in 1981, a significant factor in this turnover was an average drop of almost 10 per cent in voter turnout in these ridings.

In 1995, the Tories regained a level of support in lower-income small-town/rural ridings not seen since the late 1960s and early 1970s, winning sixteen of twenty-six ridings, many by wide margins, and 48.5 per cent of the popular vote. I have already alluded to the tendency of rural voters to re-elect incumbent MPPs for long periods, regardless of party affiliation. Except in Northern Ontario, which re-elected a number of NDP incumbents in rural seats, this pattern was broken decisively in 1995.

An interesting sidelight in this analysis involves the transformation of rural Ontario during the past generation. Agriculture now accounts for 10 per cent or more of employment in only eleven of the province's 130 ridings — ten of them in southwestern Ontario. Public service employment (government, education, health care) accounts for a larger share of the workforce than agriculture in nine of these ridings; manufacturing dominates in eight.

Shifting Patterns of Prosperity

Another possible explanation for party performance related to income is the relative improvement or decline of the economy. In the absence of current riding-level data on family incomes, the argument cannot be made conclusively. However, in comparing changes in relative household incomes between 1981 and 1991, the Tories won

Table 25 — Voting Patterns in Lower-Income Ridings (Average Household Income <85% of Ontario Average)								
	1995		1990		1987		1975-85 Average	
	#	%	#	%	#	%	#	%
Urban ridings (17)								
PC	3	28.3	0	10.9	0	12.2	3.0	30.8
Lib	8	40.0	2	33.6	12	48.6	6.5	33.3
NDP	6	31.9	15	49.5	5	37.2	7.0	38.0
Other	0	3.8	0	6.0	0	1.9	0.0	1.0
Rural/small-town ridings (24)								
PC	16	48.5	6	26.7	7	30.4	13.5	43.4
Lib	5	28.0	7	31.9	17	45.0	9.5	36.1
NDP	4	18.4	13	33.7	2	22.2	3.8	20.2
IND.	1	5.1	0	8.6	0	2.4	0.0	0.3

forty of forty-six ridings in which real household income grew more rapidly than the provincial average (22.2 per cent), but only three of the fifteen ridings that experienced marginal growth in household income during this period (see Table 26).

Although these data cover only the 1981–91 period, it should be noted that real per capita income in Ontario declined sharply during the 1990–92 recession and that federal and provincial tax increases imposed between 1990 and 1993 resulted in an even greater decline in real disposable income. While tax increases imposed by the Rae government during the recession fell disproportionately on upper-income earners, many middle-income families also experienced higher taxes, lower levels of public services, and declining living standards.

The sharpest decline in living standards was experienced by residents of inner-city industrial ridings (especially Hamilton and Sault Ste. Marie) and the resource-industry-dominated ridings of Northern Ontario. Not surprisingly, these areas looked to government for help in preserving employment levels, overwhelmingly supporting Liberal and NDP candidates, rather than blaming governments for their economic predicament.

Table 26 1995 Election Results vs. Changes in Relative Household Income: 1981-91				
1995 Election Results	PC	Lib	NDP	IND.
Real Household Income Growing Faster than Provincial Average (22.2%)	40	2	4	0
Real Household Income Growing at 90–99% of Provincial Average	36	22	9	1
Marginal Growth or Decline in Real Household Income	3	8	4	0

Ethnicity and the 1995 Election Results

Immigrants account for more than 30 per cent of the population (not necessarily voters) in twenty-eight of the thirty Metro Toronto ridings, more than 20 per cent of the population in twelve of seventeen ridings in the GTA, and in sixteen of the thirty-one ridings in other major urban areas with populations over 100,000.

While the Tories failed to win any of the six Metro ridings in which immigrants accounted for more than half of the population and won only three of nine Metro ridings with immigrant populations over 40 per cent, they won sixteen of the seventeen Metro and GTA ridings with immigrant populations between 30 and 40 percent.

Further research is needed to determine the correlation between immigrants' income levels and voting behaviour, and to analyze the preferences of immigrants of different racial and ethnic backgrounds in an election in which the NDP's employment equity laws had become a major issue.

Ridings with more than 20 per cent francophone voters, clustered primarily in northeastern Ontario and around the City of Ottawa, divided their votes mainly between the Liberals and the New Democrats.

Conclusion

The 1995 Ontario election reflects a sharp shift in the political tide. However, while the electoral basis of the Conservative majority is similar in some ways to those supporting previous majority governments in 1971 and 1981, it remains to be seen whether this electoral coalition is any more stable than its predecessors. After all, no Ontario premier has won back-to-back majority governments since John Robarts, in the 1960s.

The Conservatives restored and extended the suburban-rural coalition that was the backbone of their governing majorities during the Davis years. They enjoy strong support from upper-income and upper-middle-income constituencies, as before 1985. The most significant, but potentially volatile, addition to their coalition is composed of middle-income industrial constituencies alienated from the policies of previous Liberal and NDP governments.

The Liberals have established themselves as a predominantly urban party in the legislature, with strong support from the ridings with above-average numbers of francophones, recent immigrants, and public sector employees. They have also built a strong base in Northern Ontario. However, these gains appear to be offset by the decline of their traditional support in rural/small-town Ontario. In 1995, the Liberals retained considerable support among middle-income constituencies. Dalton McGuinty's elevation to the liberal leadership in November 1996 suggests both an effort to recover some of the party's rural/small-town base that had been largely dissipated in the 1990 and 1995 elections, and a desire to project a centrist, nonideological image likely to appeal to a broad majority of middle class voters, thus reducing the risk of ideological polarization with the Harris Tories in the next election.

The New Democrats, while deprived of many of their traditional strongholds in the 1995 election, will continue to enjoy a degree of institutional support from organized labour. They retain strong support in the resource- and government-dependent communities of Northern Ontario. Following the election of Howard Hampton as party leader in June 1996, they face the difficult challenge of reassembling the coalition between public and private sector unionized workers and their supporters in various "social movements," whose emphasis on the politics of identity has limited cultural appeal with much of the party's traditional working-class base.

The difficulty of translating constituency patterns of party preference from 1995 to subsequent elections is increased by the provincial government's decision to adopt the revised federal electoral boundaries for the next provincial election, which would reduce the number of constituencies from 130 to 103. Combined with population shifts between the 1981 and 1991 censuses, this move will result in increased representation in both absolute and relative terms for the

GTA and reduced representation for Metro Toronto, Northern Ontario, and rural/small-town areas of the province.

The Harris government's unprecedented deficit-cutting measures, which have challenged the conventional wisdom of Ontario politics by reducing public services and eroding many of the privileges and entitlements taken for granted by many voters in recent years, have moved the province into uncharted waters. Recent Ontario history cautions against making predictions of future electoral outcomes — except to suggest that one would be foolish to take the province's voters for granted.

7

Ontario's Economic Outlook

Peter Dungan

My aim in this chapter is to provide some background to the issues to be faced in governing Ontario by examining the outlook for the Ontario and Canadian economies through the next five to ten years. The work I will present has been developed by the Policy and Economic Analysis Program of the Institute for Policy Analysis. For a number of years now the Institute has been using macroeconomic computer simulation models to develop medium-term projections and investigate economic policy issues.

How We Get the Numbers

For those unfamiliar with model-based longer-term economic projections, it should be noted that the tables presented and discussed below are developed from three principal sets of ingredients.

First, a host of assumptions must be made about economic policies pursued by the different levels of government, about underlying technology and population growth, and about the future economic environment outside Canada.

Second, computer simulation models of the Canadian and Ontario economies are used to translate the assumptions into a detailed, numerical picture that allows us to make projections of output, employment, external trade, and deficits. The model contains both accounting "identities" that express the way the national accounts and other data add up and "behavioural" equations that embody our best estimate of the way segments of the economy (such as investment or consumption) have performed or behaved in the past.

Third, our own judgement is used to coordinate and make consistent the other two components. For example, initial assumptions about policy, when run through the model, may give a result that appears in our judgement to be politically unsustainable, causing us to change our assumptions. The economy remains sufficiently mysterious that the development of an economic projection is as much art as it is science.

Two additional features of this type of projection should be noted. First, the specific numbers generated by the computer model must be considered as only the middle of a range of possibilities that becomes more diffuse the further into the future we proceed. Despite the apparent precision of the numerical results, they are rough estimates only.

Second, beyond the immediate future and recovery from the current recession, the projection can only indicate trends for the future. Reality will no doubt include future business cycles, and the projection can only represent an average through the ups and downs that will inevitably occur. We do assume that the result of future cycles will likely keep the economy at a level on average below its full employment or potential level, and this feature is built into our projected longer-term trends.

Some Caveats

Several caveats are in order before we review the projections and examine their underlying themes. First, economic policy in the near future is itself subject to considerable guesswork. The federal government has now set a target of 2 per cent of gross domestic product (GDP) for the deficit of its public accounts for the fiscal year 1997–98, but the course thereafter is not known, especially because, once this deficit drops to about $10 billion, the federal government will not, in fact, be borrowing any money directly on open markets. Moreover, while Finance Minister Paul Martin likes to make "prudent" assumptions of economic growth and interest rates, we like to be prudent in our assumption of government spending: such large cuts have been announced that we think it unlikely they will all be made, especially if the economy is doing relatively poorly and deficit targets are otherwise being attained (because, say, interest rates are lower than had been prudently assumed by the Department of Finance).

A second important caveat is that some of our data for Ontario are either not very timely or subject to considerable revision. In particular, on the fiscal side, we have for Ontario nothing like the timeliness and reliability of Statistics Canada's measures of the federal fiscal situation. The figures we present on Ontario spending, revenue, and deficits therefore are, to some extent, built on an unstable foundation.

A Review of the Projections

We turn then to the projections. These are presented in detail in three tables: Table 27 is a summary of economic indicators for Ontario, Table 28 presents the major indicators for Canada, and Table 29 presents projection details for Ontario government revenues and expenditures.

First, let us review the projection numbers briefly. I should note at the outset that we are generally regarded as among the more "optimistic" of the forecasters. Of course, optimistic is a relative term. In an absolute sense, a forecast that Ontario's unemployment rate will still be at or above 7.5 per cent in 1999 is anything but optimistic, given that this rate, even in the late 1980s, was at or below 6 per cent. However, growth and employment figures such as those presented in the three tables are very hard to "sell" to most private sector forecasters or to economists on Bay Street.

Despite the fact that, technically speaking, we had a recession in Ontario in 1995 (that is, there was negative growth in each of the first two quarters), growth was actually so strong in Ontario in 1994 that the momentum carried forward into the 1995 annual growth figure. Correspondingly, the weakness in 1995 carries forward to make the 1996 annual growth number look weak at 2.6 per cent, even though growth from quarter to quarter in the year accelerates to quite an acceptable pace. Thereafter we project a number of years with growth averaging above 3.5 per cent per year (see Table 27). This figure is above the Ontario economy's potential growth rate and causes the large "output gap" (i.e., the difference between actual and potential output) left over from the 1990–92 recession to begin to close — as can be seen in the gradually declining unemployment rate. Moreover, because unemployment remains high in Ontario and Canada, this kind of growth can be achieved with inflation held firmly in check.

The forecast actually looks rosier for employment growth than fluctuations in the unemployment rate alone would suggest. The reason is that since the 1990–92 recession a large number of people have dropped out of the labour force; that is, overall labour force participation rates have dropped by several percentage points. (If

Table 27
Ontario: Economic Indicators (Base Projection, February 1996)
Summary of Projection

	1993	1994	1995	1996	1997	1998	1999	2000	2001	2002	2003	2004
Real Provincial Product (%ch)	1.3	5.5	2.6	2.6	3.9	4.0	3.7	3.6	3.5	3.4	3.2	3.3
Real GDP - Canada (%ch)	2.2	4.6	2.5	2.1	3.6	3.9	3.7	3.4	3.3	3.1	3.1	3.0
Ontario/Canada - (%)	39.5	39.9	39.9	40.1	40.2	40.3	40.3	40.3	40.4	40.5	40.6	40.7
Consumption	1.3	2.9	1.9	0.9	2.3	2.8	3.1	3.3	3.3	3.6	3.3	3.5
Government	-0.6	0.1	-0.8	-2.9	-2.3	-1.1	0.3	1.5	2.5	2.7	2.6	2.4
Private Investment	-2.1	8.9	7.7	9.2	10.4	8.6	7.4	5.9	4.7	4.0	3.7	3.5
Residential Construction	-6.8	5.0	-9.9	9.0	14.7	8.5	4.3	3.9	3.6	3.1	2.8	2.6
NonResidential Construction	-27.5	-2.2	0.8	2.5	7.2	6.3	4.9	4.0	2.9	2.7	2.6	2.5
Machinery and Equipment	11.1	13.8	17.8	10.5	9.4	9.0	9.0	7.0	5.3	4.5	4.2	4.0
Exports	8.6	12.7	9.8	6.8	7.3	6.1	4.5	4.2	3.9	3.7	3.5	3.1
Imports	8.8	11.8	11.1	4.5	6.3	5.4	4.4	4.2	3.9	3.8	3.6	3.1
Inventory - Nonfarm ($ 86 Bill)	-0.7	1.5	3.6	1.6	1.6	1.6	1.7	1.7	1.8	1.8	1.9	1.9
Inventory - Farm ($ 86 Bill)	-0.1	0.4	0.2	0.1	0.1	0.1	0.1	0.1	0.1	0.1	0.1	0.1
Residual Error ($ 86 Bill)	-1.0	-0.5	-0.5	-0.6	-0.6	-0.6	-0.6	-0.6	-0.6	-0.6	-0.6	-0.6
Nominal Gross Provincial Product (%ch)	2.0	5.2	3.1	3.5	4.9	5.3	4.9	5.0	4.8	5.1	4.7	4.9
Deflator - Ontario Gross Provincial Expenditure (%ch)	0.7	-0.4	0.4	0.9	1.0	1.2	1.2	1.3	1.3	1.6	1.4	1.5
Unemployment Rate (%)	10.6	9.6	8.7	8.6	8.4	7.9	7.6	7.2	6.8	6.6	6.4	6.2

Employment (%ch)	1.8	1.4	1.4	1.5	2.1	2.4	2.3	2.4	2.1	1.7	1.8	1.7
Employment ('000)	5090	5160	5233	5309	5422	5551	5678	5811	5934	6034	6141	6246
Labour Force (%ch)	1.5	0.2	0.5	1.3	1.8	1.9	1.9	1.9	1.7	1.5	1.5	1.5
Participation Rate	67.4	66.4	65.8	65.6	65.8	66.0	66.2	66.3	66.4	66.3	66.2	66.2
Population (%ch)	1.6	1.2	1.4	1.8	1.7	1.6	1.6	1.5	1.5	1.5	1.5	1.5
Population ('000)	10791	10925	11082	11280	11470	11654	11837	12019	12200	12382	12564	12747
Source Population (%ch)	2.0	1.7	1.5	1.5	1.5	1.7	1.6	1.7	1.6	1.6	1.6	1.6
Consumer Price Index Ontario - Inflation Rate	1.8	0.1	2.4	1.0	1.3	1.5	1.5	1.5	1.6	1.7	1.7	1.8
Annual Wage per Employee - Pvt (%ch)	-0.6	1.7	2.3	2.5	2.8	3.4	3.6	3.3	3.4	4.0	3.3	3.4
Real Ann. Wage per Emp. - Pvt (%ch)	-2.3	1.6	-0.2	1.5	1.5	1.9	2.1	1.8	1.8	2.2	1.6	1.6
Labour Productivity (%ch)	-0.5	4.1	1.2	1.1	1.7	1.6	1.4	1.2	1.3	1.7	1.4	1.5
Consolidated Government Balance ($ Bill)	-15.6	-10.1	-7.6	0.0	3.6	7.3	10.7	13.4	15.0	15.0	15.5	15.4
Federal Bal. in Ontario (National Accounts Basis) ($ Bill)	-6.2	-4.0	-3.3	2.5	5.1	7.1	9.2	11.2	12.2	12.1	12.5	11.9
Prov'l. Gov't. Balance (National Accounts Basis) ($ Bill)	-10.6	-7.4	-5.5	-3.1	-1.8	0.2	1.4	2.2	2.5	2.5	2.6	2.6
Prov'l. Balance as % of GDP	-3.7	-2.4	-1.8	-0.9	-0.5	0.1	0.4	0.6	0.6	0.6	0.6	0.5
Ratio: Prov. Debt (Accum. NA Def.) / GDP (%)	17.8	19.7	21.1	21.6	21.3	20.3	19.1	17.8	16.3	14.9	13.7	12.5
Personal Savings Rate (%)	10.2	8.9	8.0	7.5	7.7	7.7	7.7	7.7	7.9	8.3	8.4	8.6
Real Personal Disposable Income (%ch)	-1.0	1.8	0.3	0.3	2.3	2.7	3.1	3.1	3.4	3.9	3.3	3.7
Nominal After-Tax Corporate Profits (%ch)	20.0	45.1	-2.2	-0.1	25.2	15.8	5.5	4.9	3.7	4.6	5.4	5.5

Source: Focus Ontario Model: Institute for Policy Analysis

these "incipient" unemployed were actually counted as unemployed, the national unemployment rate would stand at over 12 per cent instead of at the present 9.6 per cent.) Our forecast has these "discouraged workers" coming back into the labour force in significant numbers over the next few years as further recovery takes hold, although there is a contrary opinion that much of the drop in the participation rate since 1990–92 is permanent. If these workers do return, they will keep the measured unemployment rate high even with quite respectable employment growth.

Productivity also picks up again in the projection, averaging over 1 per cent per year and thus making room for improvements in living standards. This is decent performance by historical standards but far from the increases achieved in the 1960s and early 1970s.

Where does this growth come from in terms of aggregate demand for goods and services? There are some worrisome issues here that sometimes test our optimism. For the next several years consumption is not a growth leader, although there is some help from the Ontario tax cut, which the government is phasing in. In our view, the weakness in consumption is not primarily a result of weak consumer confidence or of consumers not spending. A glance at the personal savings rate for either Ontario or Canada will show that it has been falling in recent years, indicating that consumers are spending more of their incomes, not less. No, the source of weak consumption is weak disposable income, and until employment or wage growth rebounds, or there are further tax cuts, consumption will continue to be dragged along behind GDP growth and not push it ahead.

Government spending is also not spurring demand. Note that the government spending component of GDP consists not of transfers to persons but rather of spending on civil servants and purchases of goods and services. For the next several years, this component of GDP is expected to show a significant decline, which will retard, not advance, GDP growth. By the year 2000, however, we expect a turnaround based on both pent-up demand for government services from a still-growing population and an easing of the deficit problem that will make it hard for the government to resist calls for more spending.

The factors that lead GDP growth are investment and net exports. The investment numbers have already been extremely strong for the last several years, primarily in machinery and equipment. We also foresee a continuation of the major increase in housing investment that began in 1996. This is one area where lack of confidence can be blamed for low growth in the recent past, since mortgage rates, housing prices, and demographics all argue that housing investment should be higher than it is. We find that still-lower mortgage rates achieved in early 1996, pent-up demand, and a reduction of uncertainty as government axes finally fall will all work together to boost investment in housing.

Net export growth is also crucial to our optimistic projection. The economies of Canada and Ontario are now extremely competitive due to present exchange rates, labour costs, and productivity. Restructuring and adjustment to the Canada-U.S. Free Trade Agreement have been paying off since 1994 and are expected to continue to do so. However, it is also a danger to have so much growth concentrated in investment and net exports. These are very volatile demand categories, and they make the growth path risky.

Nonetheless, our optimism regarding growth naturally leads to some good news with respect to the provincial deficit. There were some important improvements in 1995. There was less improvement in 1996, despite the spending cuts, because tax cuts also took place, and major reductions in federal transfers had to be absorbed. However, these were one-time adjustments, and, in 1997, strong real growth and continued spending constraint will pull the deficit significantly lower. We actually anticipate a near-balanced budget by 1998 on the basis of financial requirements (the public accounts deficit that normally appears in the budgets is several billion dollars higher), and we foresee further improvements thereafter. Once the debt-to-GDP ratio has peaked (in 1997, by our debt measures), the debt-deficit dynamic will begin to work in favour of reducing, not increasing, the deficit. In other words, a fall in the debt-to-GDP ratio lowers interest payments on the debt (relative to GDP) in the next year, resulting in a lower deficit, which lowers the debt ... and so on, in a virtuous cycle that is the mirror image of the vicious debt-deficit cycle that makes deficits so intractable when the debt-to-GDP ratio is rising. While we hardly dare mention it, the downward debt-to-deficit cycle at both the federal and provincial levels is so strong that we believe that, probably not much past the year 2000, large surpluses will begin to occur, and there will be room for spending increases or additional large cuts in personal income tax. (We think the tax cuts are politically the most likely outcome.)

Table 28
Canada: Economic Indicators (Base Projection, January 1996)

	1993	1994	1995	1996	1997	1998	1999	2000	2001	2002	2003	2004
Real Gross Domestic Product (% change)	2.2	4.6	2.5	2.1	3.6	3.8	3.7	3.4	3.3	3.1	3.1	3.0
Expenditure on Personal Consumption	1.6	3.0	1.6	1.2	2.5	3.1	3.2	3.0	3.3	3.2	3.6	3.5
Expenditure by Governments	0.5	-0.8	-0.4	-2.2	-1.7	-0.4	1.1	2.3	2.9	2.8	2.7	2.5
Investment Expenditure	0.5	7.5	1.0	6.9	9.6	7.8	6.6	4.7	3.6	3.1	2.4	2.2
Residential Construction	-4.2	3.0	-11.8	8.2	12.2	8.1	5.6	4.0	3.5	3.0	2.7	2.5
Non-Residential Construction	0.5	5.2	-0.8	5.0	7.8	5.7	4.3	3.1	2.5	2.0	1.7	1.5
Machinery and Equipment	3.9	11.6	9.7	7.2	9.2	8.6	8.0	5.7	4.0	3.5	2.5	2.3
Exports	10.4	14.2	11.1	7.3	8.2	6.7	6.0	5.0	4.7	4.4	3.9	3.7
Imports	8.8	10.5	8.5	5.0	6.8	5.8	5.7	4.7	4.7	4.5	4.0	3.8
Inventory - Nonfarm ($ 86 Bill)	0.1	2.8	5.2	2.6	2.5	2.6	2.7	2.8	2.9	3.0	3.1	3.1
Inventory - Farm ($ 86 Bill)	1.0	-0.1	0.7	0.6	0.4	0.2	0.2	0.2	0.2	0.2	0.2	0.2
Residual Error ($ 86 Bill)	-2.1	-0.9	-0.8	-0.3	-0.3	-0.3	-0.3	-0.3	-0.3	-0.3	-0.3	-0.3
Gross Domestic Product (%ch)	3.3	5.2	4.3	3.3	4.7	5.2	5.1	4.9	4.7	4.7	4.6	4.6
Implicit Price Deflator for GDP (%ch)	1.0	0.6	1.7	1.2	1.1	1.3	1.3	1.4	1.4	1.6	1.5	1.6
Unemployment Rate	11.2	10.4	9.5	9.5	9.2	8.6	8.2	7.8	7.4	7.2	7.2	7.1
Employment (%ch)	1.4	2.1	1.6	1.2	2.1	2.4	2.2	2.2	1.9	1.5	1.3	1.3
Labour Force (%ch)	1.3	1.1	0.7	1.1	1.7	1.8	1.7	1.7	1.5	1.2	1.3	1.2
Source Population (%ch)	1.8	1.5	1.4	1.4	1.5	1.5	1.5	1.5	1.4	1.4	1.3	1.3
Participation Rate	65.6	65.3	64.8	64.7	64.8	65.0	65.1	65.3	65.3	65.2	65.2	65.1
Finance Co. 90-Day Paper Rate	5.0	5.7	7.2	5.5	5.3	5.3	5.2	5.1	5.1	5.1	5.1	5.1

Industrial Bond Rate	8.8	9.4	9.0	7.7	7.6	7.3	7.2	6.9	6.7	6.7	6.7	6.8
Inflation Rate - CPI	1.8	0.2	2.2	1.1	1.3	1.5	1.5	1.5	1.6	1.7	1.7	1.8
Annual Wage per Employee - Pvt (%ch.)	0.6	1.5	1.7	2.1	2.9	3.6	3.6	3.3	3.5	4.0	3.9	3.8
Real Ann. Wage per Emp. - Pvt (%ch)	-1.2	1.3	-0.5	1.0	1.6	2.1	2.0	1.8	1.9	2.2	2.2	2.0
Labour Productivity (%ch)	0.8	2.4	0.9	0.9	1.5	1.4	1.5	1.2	1.3	1.6	1.8	1.6
Exchange Rate (US $/Cdn $)	0.775	0.732	0.729	0.730	0.732	0.735	0.738	0.742	0.746	0.750	0.754	0.759
Terms of Trade (%ch)	0.3	0.5	1.8	0.4	0.0	0.0	0.0	0.0	0.0	0.0	0.0	0.0
Balance on Current Account ($ Bill)	-28.8	-22.3	-16.0	-8.0	-1.1	5.0	9.5	14.0	17.7	21.4	25.1	29.0
Consolidated Government Balance ($ Bill)	-51.8	-39.4	-30.9	-17.1	-8.6	0.4	7.4	13.3	15.9	17.9	17.8	17.3
Federal Gov't Balance (NA Basis) ($ Bill)	-35.1	-28.5	-24.2	-11.6	-5.2	0.0	5.2	9.4	11.1	10.6	11.9	10.4
Federal Balance as % of GDP	-4.9	-3.8	-3.1	-1.4	-0.6	0.0	0.6	1.0	1.1	1.0	1.1	0.9
Ratio: Federal Debt to GDP (%)	51.6	53.1	54.3	54.6	53.0	50.6	47.8	44.8	41.8	38.9	36.2	33.6
Prov'l. Gov't. Balance (NA Basis) ($ Bill)	-18.2	-12.3	-8.2	-6.3	-3.6	0.8	2.5	4.1	4.5	6.7	5.0	5.0
Personal Savings Rate (%)	9.4	7.8	7.1	6.4	6.6	6.6	6.6	6.6	6.8	7.0	7.2	7.4
Real Personal Disposable Income (%ch)	0.3	1.6	0.6	0.3	2.5	2.9	3.1	2.9	3.4	3.3	3.6	3.6
Nominal After-Tax Corporate Profits (%ch)	64.4	51.8	15.7	9.6	22.6	13.0	8.7	6.3	4.1	3.7	4.1	4.0
U.S. Real GDP Growth	3.1	4.1	3.3	2.5	2.6	2.7	2.4	2.8	2.6	2.2	2.2	2.2
U.S. Inflation (GDP Deflator)	2.2	2.1	1.7	2.0	1.9	2.1	2.3	2.4	2.5	2.7	2.7	2.9
U.S. 3-Month Commercial Paper Rate	3.2	4.7	6.0	5.3	5.1	5.1	5.0	4.9	4.9	4.9	4.9	4.9

Source: Focus Ontario Model: Institute for Policy Analysis

TABLE 29
Ontario: Revenues and Expenditures (Base Projection, February 1996)
Summary of Projection

	1993	1994	1995	1996	1997	1998	1999	2000	2001	2002	2003	2004
Millions of Dollars												
Total Revenues	45569	48698	50354	50449	50382	51814	53733	55768	57902	59886	61761	63583
	(6.20)	(6.87)	(3.40)	(0.19)	(-0.13)	(2.84)	(3.70)	(3.79)	(3.83)	(3.43)	(3.13)	(2.95)
Indirect Taxes	13980	15333	15939	16654	17570	18616	19691	20814	21972	23255	24307	25397
	(3.17)	(9.68)	(3.95)	(4.49)	(5.50)	(5.95)	(5.78)	(5.70)	(5.57)	(5.84)	(4.53)	(4.48)
Direct Taxes - Corp & Gov't Bus Ent	2162	2640	3219	3407	3823	4134	4258	4376	4461	4588	4739	4926
	(5.00)	(22.12)	(21.93)	(5.83)	(12.21)	(8.14)	(2.98)	(2.78)	(1.94)	(2.85)	(3.30)	(3.94)
Direct Taxes & Transfers from Persons	17489	18791	18666	18677	17907	18223	18956	19626	20203	20394	20670	20806
	(2.69)	(7.45)	(-0.67)	(0.06)	(-4.13)	(1.77)	(4.02)	(3.54)	(2.94)	(0.95)	(1.35)	(0.66)
Investment Income	2931	3137	3342	3454	3559	3666	3787	3912	4055	4204	4357	4516
	(9.53)	(7.04)	(6.52)	(3.36)	(3.03)	(3.01)	(3.30)	(3.30)	(3.65)	(3.65)	(3.65)	(3.65)
Other Current Transfers from Persons	1093	1105	1028	1034	1063	1106	1150	1196	1244	1293	1345	1399
Transfers from Federal Government	7879	7660	8129	7192	6430	6038	5860	5812	5936	6120	6310	6506
	(15.02)	(-2.78)	(6.12)	(-11.53)	(-10.59)	(-6.10)	(-2.94)	(-0.81)	(2.13)	(3.10)	(3.10)	(3.10)
Transfers from Municipalities	35	31	31	31	31	31	31	32	32	32	33	33
Total Expenditures	56972	56916	56744	54384	53091	52485	53265	54511	56282	58283	60171	61973

Current Exp. on Goods & Services	17170 (2.99)	16574 (3.24)	15984 (3.55)	15343 (3.25)	14803 (2.34)	14538 (1.49)	14507 (-1.14)	14974 (-2.38)	15745 (-4.16)	16478 (-0.30)	16722 (-0.10)	16919 (2.04)
Gross Capital Formation	1674, (3.60,) (3.46)	1618 (3.69) (3.37)	1565 (4.18) (3.66)	1510 (3.65) (3.30)	1461 (1.82) (3.14)	1417 (0.22) (2.24)	1386 (-3.12) (1.59)	1364 (-4.90) (0.57)	1356 (-4.45) (0.83)	1345 (-1.46) (7.53)	1251 (-1.16) (6.02)	1180 (1.75) (1.99)
Transfers to Persons	11507 (2.58)	11218 (2.58)	10936 (2.58)	10661 (2.58)	10393 (2.08)	10181 (2.08)	9973 (0.39)	9934 (-1.40)	10075 (-5.21)	10628 (-1.54)	10794 (1.01)	10686 (-2.14)
Subsidies	786 (2.50)	767 (2.50)	748 (2.50)	730 (2.50)	712 (1.00)	705 (0.10)	704 (-3.02)	726 (-5.01)	764 (-4.15)	793 (-14.72)	935 (-9.99)	1039 (-15.67)
Interest on the Public Debt	10976 (1.59)	10805 (1.66)	10628 (1.69)	10451 (1.70)	10277 (2.04)	10071 (2.57)	9819 (3.45)	9492 (4.86)	9052 (6.70)	8483 (6.53)	7963 (7.26)	7424 (20.79)
Capital Assistance	371	360	350	339	329	320	315	314	315	304	80	286
Transfers to Muns. & Hosps.	19486 (3.50)	18826 (4.19)	18069 (4.77)	17246 (4.29)	16537 (3.15)	16032 (1.58)	15783 (-3.11)	16290 (-4.62)	17079 (-8.71)	18709 (-2.40)	19170 (-1.38)	19438 (-0.18)
Capital Consumption Allowances	983	961	942	925	911	899	890	882	875	868	863	848
Surplus (+) or Deficit (-) : NA Basis	2593 (42)	2551 (7)	2544 (0)	2545 (377)	2167 (800)	1367 (1149)	219 (2045)	-1826 (1234)	-3060 (2461)	-5521 (1833)	-7354 (3201)	-10555 (1548)
Debt : NA Basis	59387 (-2632)	62019 (-2556)	64574 (-2550)	67124 (-2574)	69698 (-1852)	71550 (-904)	72455 (481)	71974 (2442)	69532 (3703)	65829 (6220)	59609 (8541)	51068 (11397)
Surplus (+) or Deficit (-) : PA Basis	132, (74)	58 (8)	50 (0)	51 (385)	-334 (808)	-1142 (1132)	-2274 (2171)	-4445 (1734)	-6179 (2829)	-9008 (908)	-9916 (149)	-10066 (1988)
Debt : PA Basis	101679 (-194)	101873 (-65)	101938 (-57)	101994 (-57)	102051 (344)	101708 (1157)	100551 (2266)	98285 (4437)	93848 (6171)	87677 (9006)	78671 (9916)	68755 (10066)

Note - Percentage changes (or changes in levels) in parentheses. Source: Focus Ontario Model: Institute for Policy Analysis

Grounds for Optimism

What grounds do we have for suggesting that such a relatively optimistic view of the future is possible? There are at least four interrelated elements of our optimism (on each of which, of course, economists disagree).

The first element is our estimate of the potential growth of the economy. For Canada, our estimate of underlying potential growth is about 3 per cent per year, and for Ontario it is several tenths of a percentage point higher due to Ontario's more rapid population growth and more extensive restructuring. The most contentious part of this estimate is the productivity component; there is a wide body of opinion on past and future potential growth rates, and we are definitely on the high side.

The second element behind our optimism is our estimate of the current output gap. If you accept that the Ontario economy's potential has been growing at 3 per cent or more per year since 1989, then at present Ontario is producing perhaps 10 per cent or more below its potential. With a gap this large, it would be possible for Ontario to grow at one or two percentage points above its 3 per cent potential for a number of years and still not fully close the gap or put any serious pressure on inflation.

The third element of optimism is an understanding (or perhaps faith or belief) that economies close their output gaps; that there are natural equilibrating forces at work to reduce excess supplies of labour and capital and get the economy back to work. The process may work slowly, perhaps, but the movement appears to be inevitable unless the economy is continually restrained from reaching its potential by policy errors. This understanding was borne out in the recovery from the recession of 1981–82. At the time and in the years immediately after, there was much talk of the unemployment rate staying high and of no new sources of economic demand or jobs. As it turned out, the mid-1980s saw growth well in excess of potential; the unemployment rate fell gradually, but quite substantially. The forecasts we were developing in 1983–85 were considered optimistic by many economists at the time, but these economists seriously underforecast the level that GDP finally attained by 1989. (Of course, we also did not forecast the made-in-Canada recession of the early 1990s. As a result, our forecasts in 1984 for the 1995 GDP pretty much hit on the mark, but with sizable over- and under-estimates on the way!)

The fourth element of optimism is that, with one possible exception, the policy settings now appear to be correct. This is especially true of the Bank of Canada's inflation target of 1 to 3 per cent, which we assume will be maintained past the year 2000. If the output gap fails to close, the inflation rate will fall, and the Bank will probably be forced to ease monetary policy and allow the dollar to drop until growth is restimulated. The Bank overestimated the strength of the Canadian economy in 1994 and tightened monetary policy prematurely (although it also had to contend with the Quebec Referendum). In effect, the Bank was trying for a soft landing before the Canadian economy had even left the ground. We expect that, with this lesson learned, the Bank will be more careful in the future.

Fiscal policy, too, is largely on the right course. The deficit problem needs to be addressed — not too quickly and not too slowly. At present, we believe the deficit should be addressed with spending cuts and patience, not with tax increases and certainly not with inflationary tax increases such as sales tax hikes or payroll taxes. Appropriate attention is being paid to efficiency and to the proper division of tasks between the private and public sectors. Mistakes will no doubt be made, but the goals are correct and should serve to increase efficiency, productivity growth, and capital formation and contribute to higher output that is more balanced and sustainable.

A Final Concern

Fiscal policy is, however, a source of one final concern with which I close. Major government cutbacks are ahead for Canada and Ontario in 1997–98. Our work indicates that net exports and new investment (in areas such as housing) can grow sufficiently strongly in this period both to close the output gap somewhat and to make up for the demand that is being taken out of the system by government cutbacks. But there is a massive shift of economic resources taking place beneath the surface, with both labour and capital being deployed out of production for government and consumption and into production for export, import replacement, or investment. The economy has the capacity to make impressive shifts. Already narrow public sector employment has declined by over 100,000 jobs from mid-1994 levels. Since there has been a net increase in the number of jobs created over the same interval, the private sector must have created well over 100,000 new positions. But adjustment can proceed only so far and so fast, and it is possible that, in Ontario especially, the combined federal and provincial cuts planned for the next two years may be too great for the economy to absorb all at once — in which case we are facing lower growth and higher unemployment than we have projected in this paper. Almost certainly, when it comes to cuts in the next two years, we can do no more than is currently planned. Nor should we, for these projections indicate that the current fiscal plans, if carried out, will set us firmly on the road to deficit correction. For the next while, at both federal and provincial levels, the watchwords on deficit reduction must be *creativity* and *patience* — and not *cuts*.

8

Transition: The Tories Take Power

Graham White

The 1995 Ontario election marked the first time in living memory that virtually all political observers and participants expected the government to change. Accordingly, for the first time, politicians and bureaucrats alike devoted considerable time and energy to transition planning — attempting to ensure a smooth transfer of power from the New Democrats to their successors. Against all odds, the NDP's successors turned out not to be Lyn McLeod's Liberals, who had long enjoyed a massive lead in the polls, but Mike Harris's Conservatives — the Common Sense Revolutionaries.

This remarkable turn of events might well have made for a highly problematic transition. The Tory transition, however, proved remarkably smooth and effective and offers valuable lessons for others who may find themselves involved in similar exercises. This paper presents an overview of research that my colleague, David Cameron, and I conducted into the 1995 transition.[1] Its primary objective is to account for the success of the Tory transition. A subtheme is the restoration of the old bureaucratic guard, which accompanied the transition.

Transition, I should clarify, is a term that encompasses only one aspect of what a new government does in its early days (indeed, primarily in the days before it formally takes office). It refers to a party's taking over the levers of power and getting into a position to make decisions; it is not about the decisions themselves. Transition entails not only key personnel choices — most notably, ministers and their staffs — but also issues of organizational design, such as the cabinet decision-making process and the structure and jurisdiction of ministries, as well as the issue of establishing a working relationship with the bureaucracy, particularly at the senior levels.

Of course, for a very long period, transition was a nonissue in Ontario, since governments simply have not changed. From World War II until the 1980s, mounting a research project on Ontario transitions would have been roughly equivalent to studying the palm trees of Baffin Island. The 1995 transition was the third in a decade — how the eternal verities of Ontario politics have been shaken! — but it proved qualitatively different from the Liberal transition in 1985 and the NDP transition in 1990. The Liberals experienced a smooth transition, but its success owed as much to good luck as to good management. The NDP transition, which one key participant called "the transition from hell," featured a party with no governing experience but with an ambitious agenda for change, thrust without warning into office. Once in office, the NDP encountered a bureaucracy unprepared for serious political change; the whole process was suffused with deep mistrust and ignorance on both sides of the political-bureaucratic divide.[2]

Much the same dynamic, resulting in a similarly difficult transition, might have been expected when Mike Harris and his Common Sense Revolution team won the 1995 election. Although some personnel errors were made, some flawed organizational designs adopted, and some mistakes made in relations with the public service, overall the Tory transition was highly successful. In a short time and with remarkably few serious problems, the Conservatives had convincingly taken over the reins of power.

Why did this transition work so well? Quite simply, both the bureaucrats and the politicians were well prepared. Not only had they seen to the mundane nuts and bolts, but they had thought through the larger questions that arise when governments change.

Bureaucratic Preparations

It is understandable why political parties that go into elections with little expectation of winning (as was the case with both the Liberals in 1985 and the NDP in 1990) don't devote much time to transition planning. It's less understandable why that would happen on the bureaucratic side; nonetheless, this is in fact what happened prior to 1995. In 1985 and 1990 almost no bureaucratic preparations were made for the possibility of a change in government. Doubtless this reflected the incumbent governments' standing of more than 50 per cent in the polls when they went to the hustings (historically, in

Ontario's three-party system a majority government requires only 43 or 44 per cent of the vote). When David Cameron and I were interviewing bureaucrats prior to the 1995 election about their transition planning, I was struck by how many of them seemed to be reading Donald Savoie's book *Taking Power: Managing Government Transitions*, a collection that constitutes virtually the corpus of Canadian academic literature on transitions. As a political scientist, I found it heartening that important people in government take the work of political scientists seriously and that our views and research could be of practical use. At the same time, as the author of the Ontario chapter in the book, I was taken aback that the Ontario government possessed so little in the way of chronicles and assessments of previous transitions that Savoie's book (and my piece in it) turned up on so many key bureaucrats' desks.

From all reports, one of the prime forces energizing the bureaucratic transition planning was Premier Rae's sense of having been very shabbily treated in the 1990 transition. In part, this bad experience occurred at the political level; some in the NDP spoke of just about everything, apart from manuals for the photocopy machines, being shredded. More pervasive among the New Democrats, though, was a strong sense that they had not been well served, or indeed treated fairly, by the public service. Rae was determined that the debacle of the 1990 transition would not be repeated and therefore insisted on a competent, professional transition to the new government.

Leadership of this exercise fell to Cabinet Secretary David Agnew, who had been Rae's principal secretary in 1990 and had thus experienced the transition from a political perspective. Agnew set in motion the first comprehensive transition planning process in Ontario bureaucratic history. He met with federal bureaucrats, including former cabinet secretaries, to gain firsthand knowledge of transition planning in Ottawa; he and his staff also met with the opposition transition teams.

In the cabinet office, Agnew established a small team to supervise and direct transition planning. In turn, this group set up a committee composed of representatives from all "line" ministries (that is, ministries that deliver programs and services to the public) who acted as conduits for line ministry involvement in the process; they advised the cabinet office, disseminated directives and information from the centre (that is, from central agencies such as the Premier's office, cabinet office and ministry of finance), and coordinated ministry responses. They developed standard information protocols for ministries to supply to the centre. This information was processed into standardized briefing books to be handed to the new government's political transition team. The cabinet office team also looked after routine logistical matters, such as ensuring that the incoming political transition team had sufficient office space in a good location, with computers, phone lines, fax machines, and other necessary amenities and facilities. Unexceptional as any of this might seem, none of it was provided to the political transition teams in 1985 or 1990.

Contrary to what might have been expected, the cabinet office's exercises involving information gathering and processing neither analyzed nor estimated the costs of the promises in the Liberal Red Book or the Conservatives' Common Sense Revolution. Instead, this estimating took place to some extent within individual ministries. The cabinet office aimed instead at basic information akin to Ministry of XYZ 101: what the ministry does, its legal framework (the statutes it administers), organizational structure, budget, and principal short- and long-term issues. For the first time, an incoming government received a standardized, comprehensive set of briefing books organized by ministry. Like the provision of office space and equipment, this process may not seem noteworthy, but it marked a clear departure from the norm. Some of the material assembled by the cabinet office was used extensively by the Conservative transition team; some was not.

One of the unusual features of this process was the way it flew in the face of the strong culture of decentralization within the public service sector. In Ontario, line ministries traditionally are reluctant to provide extensive operational information to the centre. In our research we repeatedly encountered suspicion about the cabinet office's demands for information. To some extent, this was simply garden-variety grumbling about the effort required to assemble, tabulate, and present the information in a one-size-fits-all format. More problematic was a related "why do they want to know this?" attitude within line ministries. In part this was a reflection of the generic disdain in all governments for central agencies, but in another sense, *they* was code for David Agnew and his presumed NDP fellow travellers. In other words, there was some suspicion that information was being sought for untoward political purposes. Still, although the Cabinet Office transition planners encountered some obstacles, in the end, ministries did provide the required information in the prescribed form.

The material assembled at the centre was primarily designed for the use of the party transition team, though incoming ministers would also see their ministries' binders. Most ministries also put together extensive additional material for their ministers, providing far more detail than was available through the central process. The principles that guided the content and the presentation of briefing books for each ministry varied substantially.

Of course, largely because no one had expected the government to change in 1985 or 1990, this extensive preparation and the resulting standardized briefing material represented an important first step. In contrast, the material hastily put together for the new Liberal and NDP governments was very uneven, and from the New Democrats' point of view, quite unsatisfactory.

The product of the transition planning exercise — the information in the briefing books — was obviously valuable, but so too was the process itself. It succeeded in focusing the attention and the thinking of the public service on the coming transition and sent out a clear message that the bureaucracy had better be prepared for it. The real test of the bureaucracy's preparedness, of course, lay in implementing the new government's policy agenda, but a concern with preparation was also manifested in apparently trivial things that we were told repeatedly meant a good deal, both symbolically and substantively, to the incoming government. These were things as simple as having parking spaces and permits ready for the minister and the minister's staff and having the minister's name on the door within minutes of the swearing-in. When ministers first arrived at their offices, whether on the afternoon of the swearing-in or the next day, their names had already been emblazoned not just on their office doors, but also in the entranceways to their buildings.

Another positive side effect of the extensive bureaucratic preparations for transition can't be pursued here but does warrant passing mention. This was the way that more-astute deputy ministers used the process not just to prepare for a new government, but for strategic planning and evaluation purposes.

Political Preparations

On the political side, I will deal only with the Conservatives.[3] One of the most significant and surprising elements about the Tories' transition planning is that a party that had been mired for years more than twenty points behind the front-running Liberals should devote any attention at all to transition concerns. Yet as early as the Conservatives' 1992 Windsor Convention, the party's strategic plan, "Mission '97," included a commitment to "complete the development of a detailed, integrated transition strategy six months prior to the next election."[4] And although transition planning may not have been at the top of the Tory agenda in the run-up to the election, the commitment to it was by no means set aside, for serious work was under way for more than a year before the election was called.

In both their election planning and their policy goals, the Conservatives were clearly focused about what they wanted to do and how they would go about doing it. They understood that to be able to bring about the sweeping policy changes they desired, they would have to have their hands firmly on the levers of power without delay after winning power.

The Common Sense Revolution — Harris's policy proposals, released well in advance of the election — was an important element in the Conservatives' transition process. This was no mere election gimmick; the Conservatives truly believed in it. As such, it provided a blueprint for action and guidance for governing, with its overriding emphasis on deficit reduction. Once in power, there would be no dithering over what to do. The questions facing a Harris government would not be about policy — the proposals settled that — but about implementation. This in turn emphasized the importance of a well-managed transition.

David Lindsay, Harris's principal secretary — his key political aide — and retired business executive Bill Farlinger, a close Harris adviser, established a small transition planning team. This was a rather loose grouping with various people moving in and out of the team, though as the election neared the group did become somewhat more formal and structured. Although it included politicos from the Davis era with links to the Mulroney government, it depended heavily on several former Ontario deputy ministers.

One important factor that contributed to the success of the transition was the explicit decision that the transition planning exercise be kept almost entirely separate from the election planning and implementation process. Thus the transition team was able to beaver away on issues of government structure, management, relations with the bureaucracy, and the like, in splendid isolation from the politicians and their advisers on the campaign buses, who were totally absorbed with the election. Only at the top, through David Lindsay, were transition preparation and campaign management linked, and even at that level, Lindsay delegated most of the transition work once the campaign was under way.

Once the results were in, the separation between those with political responsibilities and those working on transition continued. A small number of people, centred around Harris and Lindsay, saw to policy decisions that had to be made quickly and dealt with media and communications issues — in short, they handled the politics. By and large, the central figures in the campaign retained their political roles in the government-in-waiting. The transition team didn't get into politics or policy; they simply dealt with the nuts and bolts of taking over a government and trying to manage relations with the public service. A central element in its work was ensuring that the key political players were not distracted from their political tasks by routine, yet essential, questions of management and organization.

Clearly, the Tories' success in the transition owed a good deal to their very able, experienced transition team. The former deputies and the politicos on the team brought a wealth of practical experience with government. Significantly, private sector business types who did not have extensive firsthand experience in government were a decided minority among the dozen members of the formal transition team.

Also noteworthy was the fact that virtually all those on the transition team took on their duties — for which they were not paid — with the firm conviction that they did not want government jobs. They came to work on a limited project, with no intention of staying on in the premier's office or elsewhere in the new government. And indeed, by the time of the swearing-in, less than three weeks after the election, all but one had returned to private life. An obvious advantage of this arrangement was that the transition was not managed by people whose actions might have been guided by considerations of future personal involvement — of where they might fit in the political pecking order, for example. The arrangement did, however, have the disadvantages of a transition team lacking in long-term ownership and responsibility for its work and insensitive to the principle of keeping low-level concerns off the key politicos' plates. Particularly as the swearing-in approached, bureaucrats who sought directions or decisions from a transition team member were told, "I won't be here next week; you'd better ask David Lindsay." Indeed, although the way in which the transition was structured removed a great many details from the purview of Harris's key political staff, a serious bottleneck did emerge early on, in which too many decisions were required of the few people close to Harris.

The Tories were also lucky. It was summer, and with the election out of the way most people had better things to do than to pay close attention to politics. Moreover, to the extent that anyone was watching politics, the focus was on the run-up to the Quebec Referendum. Accordingly, the Tories had the luxury of being able to go about their transition with little scrutiny from the media or from the public.

The Tories by no means ran a flawless transition. Insufficient resources were devoted to the mammoth and critical task of recruiting ministerial staff; the resulting process was more ad hoc than was desirable. Similarly, the nascent premier's office was too thin on the ground: the political staff around Harris were experienced and capable, but they were simply too few in number. This exacerbated the bottleneck that would come later.

In addition, a certain amount of wheel-reinventing occurred. The briefing books, so laboriously prepared by the bureaucrats, often sat unopened for long stretches of time. Ministers and their political staff repeatedly asked the bureaucrats for material that was already in their briefing books. It took some time for the transition teams and the new ministers to recognize the utility of the material the bureaucrats had prepared. Similarly, some of the work done by the transition team in setting up seminars for ministers and MPPs duplicated work that had already been done by the bureaucrats.

All told, however, these problems were little more than hiccups in a strikingly successful operation. Quickly and effectively, the Tories placed themselves in a position to carry out their political agenda. This readiness is noteworthy in view of the limited experience among the new ministers. Only a few had any cabinet experience, and even those, including Harris and Finance Minister Ernie Eves, had generally held only minor portfolios for brief periods in 1985, under Frank Miller.

The Conservatives deserve full marks for a very successful transition and for taking seriously the need for good transition planning even when their prospects for victory seemed slight. The Tories' advance work would not have paid such handsome dividends, however, without the thorough, effective preparations and the operational and mental readiness for transition of the bureaucrats. Indeed, members of the Tory transition team we interviewed were effusive in their praise of David Agnew. They described him as highly professional and extremely helpful, and they readily acknowledged his contribution to the effectiveness of the transition. This is particularly telling because it contrasted so sharply with the comments of senior bureaucrats, at least those who retained their jobs under the new government.

Bureaucratic Restoration

This leads directly into an important sidebar to the 1995 Ontario transition — the restoration to prominence of particular figures within the Ontario public service who embody a set of bureaucratic values that were to an extent displaced during the NDP regime.

Both the Conservative and Liberal transition teams assigned high priority to management of the relationship between the politicians and the bureaucrats. Both teams saw this as central to their prospects for successfully implementing their policy agendas. They also saw this relationship as having been especially problematic for the NDP government. They further believed that during its time in office, the NDP had politicized the public service to an unprecedented and dangerous degree. Many in the public service agreed.

This was a widely held perception, but it is not an easy claim to substantiate. Certainly the NDP brought to office a perspective on the nature and role of bureaucracy that differed from that of their predecessors. It was not that they appointed party hacks to sensitive bureaucratic posts or engaged in rampant patronage. Rather, their break with the past raised more fundamental questions. In particular, the question arose as to whether a party seeking fundamental social change requires a senior bureaucracy that understands and supports its ideological underpinnings. The NDP argued that traditional bureaucratic political neutrality actually meant nonpartisanship in the sense of refraining from favouring one party over another; this definition did not extend to more basic ideological orientations. Indeed, many in the NDP saw the senior bureaucracy as the establishment, intent on blocking progressive political change. The NDP's practical response to this theory of bureaucratic engagement was to appoint and promote a number of senior public servants who had either links to the party or experience working for NDP governments in western Canada.

Previous Conservative and Liberal governments had, of course, brought into senior bureaucratic posts a good many party supporters or ideological soulmates. Politicization in this form is more easily identified and more readily dealt with than the transformation the NDP wrought in the upper reaches of the bureaucracy. The merits and demerits of politicization of the public service are not the issue here, nor is the quality of the NDP appointments — though it should be recognized that many of the key NDP appointees, such as Michael Mendelson, the deputy cabinet secretary, and Jay Kaufman, the finance deputy, were career bureaucrats who had been brought into the Ontario public service under the Liberals.

Within the Conservative party and among a significant old guard of deputy ministers (and former deputy ministers who had left government early in the NDP mandate), it had become an article of faith that the public service had been sullied and politicized by the NDP. Putting this situation to rights was a high Tory priority.

A key first step, both operationally and symbolically, towards "depoliticizing" the public service was Harris's announcement, less than a week after the election, that he would be appointing Rita Burak to replace David Agnew as cabinet secretary. This step was neither surprising nor exceptional. Since Agnew had been a close political adviser of Premier Rae, it was inconceivable that any new government would retain him in the crucial position of cabinet secretary. Moreover, Burak was one of the most experienced, most able deputy ministers; she was widely hailed as "a bureaucrat's bureaucrat." Her appointment sent strong signals to the public service that the Tories intended to work with the existing bureaucracy and that they would emphasize a strictly nonpartisan public service. (At the press conference announcing her appointment, Burak made a point of saying that she is so apolitical as to refrain from voting.)

If Burak was unquestionably well qualified for the job, it is nonetheless telling that she embodied the return to power of the old bureaucratic guard. She herself had been sidelined by the NDP in a relatively unimportant portfolio — the Ministry of Agriculture, Food, and Rural Development — and her husband, Peter Barnes, had been removed as cabinet secretary by Rae in favour of David Agnew.

"The return to power of the old bureaucratic guard" is perhaps a less accurate way of describing the change than "the reassertion of old bureaucratic values," for only a small number of senior bureaucrats who had fallen out of favour or who had left were restored to high positions. Extensive personnel changes did take place in the senior ranks of the public service; those promoted to fill the vacancies were strong adherents to the notion of the public service as a nonpartisan, apolitical institution faithfully administering the policies of whatever party happened to form the government.

And vacancies there were. A few days before the swearing-in, a half-dozen deputy ministers were fired in a ruthless purge. Some, such as Mendelson and Kaufman and Rae's confidant Jeff Rose, a former president of the Canadian Union of Public Employees, were obvious targets. Others had solid bureaucratic track records and no partisan ties. Several more deputies were subsequently fired and, below the deputy level, there were isolated firings and reassignments of career bureaucrats who were perceived as having been too closely associated with the NDP government. All of the new deputy ministerial appointments were made from within the public service (save that of Mike Gourley, a senior administrator at the University of Western Ontario who had previously held a series of senior posts in the public service). As the Burak appointment had indicated, and the internal promotions to the vacant deputy ministerships confirmed, the new Conservative government took seriously its commitment to a politically neutral public service. Yet in other ways — particularly in its bureaucrat-bashing during the election campaign and its enthusiasm once in office for massive layoffs within the institution — it revealed deep-seated hostility towards the Ontario public service.

Whether the effectiveness and the morale of the Ontario public service — or the Conservative government's relationship and dealings with that institution — have been improved by removing political deputy ministers and ideological soulmates of the NDP and returning to a Davis-era conception of the public service is too complex an issue to be pursued here. Nor is it as straightforward as it might seem. The "politicization" of the public service under the NDP could be interpreted as simply a recognition that, as academics have long argued, it is unrealistic to expect a rigid demarcation between politics and administration at the highest reaches of the public service. Moreover, are not senior bureaucrats who are facilitating the implementation of the radical Harris agenda going beyond the professional duty of the public service to do the bidding of the duly elected government and, in effect, adopting a clearly ideological (albeit nonpartisan) posture? Can public servants, in other words, be truly neutral players in what amounts to a massive dismantling of the state?

Even framing the issue in this manner would doubtless generate extensive debate. What cannot be disputed, though, is that this phase of the transition warrants attention because of its intrinsic importance, marking as it does a sea change in the upper levels of the public service.

Conclusion

The remarkable volatility of the Ontario electorate, which has entrusted majority governments to three different parties in less than a decade, suggests that transitions and transition planning have become standard features of the province's political life. Future transitions will build upon the notable success of the 1995 Tory transition. On the bureaucratic side, it would be hard to imagine a return to the ad hoc transitions of 1985 and 1990.

Politically, a smooth, effective transition is a necessary, though not sufficient, condition for a government to be successful. (The politically damaging errors made by the Conservatives in their handling of Bill 26 — the "Omnibus Bill" — shows that even a good transition will not provide all the answers.) Particularly for a party aiming at far-reaching policy change, such as the Ontario Conservatives in 1995, a sure-handed grasp on the levers of power is essential. The story, and indeed the central lesson, of the 1995 Ontario transition is not just that bureaucrats and politicos must be well prepared for transitions, but that handsome dividends will be paid to a political party that takes seriously its responsibility to prepare to govern.

Endnotes

1. This paper is based on research conducted with Professor David Cameron of the University of Toronto, but he bears no responsibility for the views presented in it. The research primarily reflects several dozen not-for-attribution interviews with public servants and political figures; we wish to record our thanks for their time, interest, and candour.
2. For a more extended comparison of the Liberal and NDP transitions, see Graham White, "Traffic Pileups at Queen's Park: Recent Ontario Transitions," in Donald Savoie, ed., *Taking Power: Managing Government Transitions*, Toronto: Institute of Public Administration of Canada, 1993, 115–43.
3. The Liberals, of course, had been widely expected to win the election and had mounted their own transition planning exercise.
4. Progressive Conservative Party of Ontario, *Convention Participant Ideas Input Booklet*, October 1992, 8–9.

9

Queen's Park
Policy-Making Systems

David A. Wolfe

Designing an appropriate policy-making system is one of the first
and most important tasks that confronts each new government. The
challenge is to ensure that the system is relatively efficient in terms
of both the process for making decisions and the outcomes of that
process. The policy-making system must ensure a fairly steady flow
of policy outcomes that are internally consistent and that operate
within a consistent fiscal framework. At the same time, these outcomes must be responsive to the political goals and priorities of the
incoming government. Designing a policy-making system poses a
substantial challenge for any government, but is particularly difficult
for a party with no previous experience in governing. The NDP
government elected in 1990 and the PC government elected in 1995
differed dramatically in their approaches to policy-making. A careful
examination of the experiences of these governments provides in-
sights into the perils and pitfalls of designing policy-making systems.

A key problem faced by the NDP's leaders and political staff was
the fifty or more years of unmet expectations that had built up among
their supporters. For many in the party, the election result of 1990
represented a singular opportunity to deliver on those expectations.
Through its many years in opposition, the NDP had excelled at
internal policy debates and discussions, its policy resolution books
providing strong testament to this tradition. However, transforming
these resolutions into a clear and consistent set of priorities that were
fiscally feasible required quite a different set of skills. At the same
time, many in the NDP feared that existing policy and bureaucratic
structures at Queen's Park would not prove sufficiently responsive

to their political objectives. To compound these difficulties, the government had the misfortune to be elected at the onset of the worst economic recession since the 1930s, with the province facing stagnant or declining revenues for the first time since 1945.[1] This made the task of defining a coherent policy framework all the more difficult.

The policy literature in Canada is replete with discussions of the relative success or failure of governments in implementing new policy-making processes.[2] While the lessons to be drawn from this literature do not give much cause for optimism, each system should be judged on its own strengths and failings. The institutional structures and processes most pertinent to the issues considered in this discussion include the nature of the cabinet policy system, the role of central agencies, and the relationship between the policy and expenditure management processes. While these issues are common to all parliamentary governments, the variations in the way governments deal with them reveal much about the parties' nature.

Competing Pressures

Within the Westminster model of government there is a continuous tension between centralization and decentralization in the policy-making structures. A critical issue involves the degree of control exerted by the premier (and his or her political staff) over the policy system and by the finance minister over the expenditure management system. The effectiveness of the priorty-setting processes is dependent upon the degree of centralization and the degree to which priority setting has been integrated within the fiscal framework. For example, a more centralized system may result in more economically efficient outcomes by reducing the prospects for particular interests to assert their claims on scarce fiscal or policy resources. The manner in which the centralization/decentralization issue is structured in terms of cabinet decision-making is closely mirrored in the relationship between the central agencies and the "line" ministries (i.e., ministries such as Health, which deliver programs and services to the public). While noting the presence of competing pressures for both centralization and decentralization, political scientists Peter Aucoin and Herman Bakvis observe that

> The logic of centralization derives first and foremost from the need for government, as a single organizational entity, to function as a coordinated and integrated system ... there must be

an expenditure budget for the entire government if budgeting
is to cope with scarce resources; the government must endeav-
our to be as consistent as possible in its dealings with other
governments ... and the policies and programs of the government must be synchronized if there is to be anything resembling
a strategic plan to deal with the interdependencies between
policies and programs.[3]

At the same time, the literature also makes it clear that excessive
centralization of the policy process carries its own costs. Excessive
centralization may impede the ability and willingness of the line
ministries to lend their expertise in the design and implementation
of policy. A great advantage of using ministry-based expertise in the
policy-making process is the opportunity it affords to realize the
benefits of "policy learning"; that is, the cumulative knowledge built
up through past experimentation in policy design. Problems may
occur, however, if the design of policy is excessively centralized in
the policy branches of ministries to the exclusion of other branches
with experience in program administration. The exclusion of program administrators from the design of policy may also result in their
lack of commitment to the outcome of the process, thus hindering
effective implementation of the policy. At worst, an excessively
centralized system turns inward, focusing all its energies on the
design and management of the policy process itself and ultimately
losing sight of the ends it was designed to achieve.

The tension between centralization and decentralization has implications at both the political and bureaucratic levels of the policy-
making system. In other words, it has implications for both cabinet
decision-making and the supporting infrastructure of central agencies. Students of policy-making tend to emphasize the bureaucratic
dimension, but in designing the system the premier and cabinet are
frequently motivated by political considerations. In the case of the
NDP government, the principal concerns underlying the design of
the cabinet decision-making system were to impose a collective
discipline on a set of neophyte ministers and ensure that the line
ministries responded to the priorities set through the system. It is easy
to confuse this desire to maintain coherence and political control with
a desire to politicize the public service. The Ontario public service
had long enjoyed an extraordinary tradition of bureaucratic decentralization, with far weaker control by central agencies than had been
established at the federal level in the 1960s. Therefore, the old line

bureaucrats who reacted negatively to the NDP's changes (as Graham White notes in the preceding chapter) may have been reacting more to the NDP's assertion of central control over the policy system than to the making of an excessive number of political appointments at senior bureaucratic levels, since relatively few such appointments were actually made.

Design of the NDP System

Premier Rae and his key advisers were faced with a number of options for the initial design of the policy-making system. Much of the work carried out during the 1990 transition focused on the experiences of the Blakeney government in Saskatchewan and the Schreyer government in Manitoba. Both of these governments had created a planning secretariat that reported directly to the Planning and Priorities Committee of the cabinet. The secretariat's task was to define government's long-term policy priorities and objectives. Among some of the key advisers engaged in the Ontario transition there was a strong conviction that the planning secretariat was the best option, since it could be staffed by a mix of career civil servants and advisers from outside the government. The advantages of this approach, its supporters believed, were that it would help to maintain close links between the government and its political base in the party, and that it would help to allay the fears of many in the party that the government would be "captured" by the bureaucracy or its initiatives thwarted by bureaucratic foot-dragging. However, other advisers believed that the planning secretariats in Saskatchewan and Manitoba had become too powerful and all-encompassing, with the consequence that they stifled the capacities of the line ministries to develop policies. From this perspective, a more desirable approach was to enhance the priority-setting role of the Policy and Priorities (P&P) Board of the cabinet and to ensure that the overall structure of policy committees in cabinet was well supported by a strong policy capacity in the central agencies. In the end, Rae opted for the latter approach and expanded the capacity for policy-making and analysis within the cabinet office, rather than creating a separate secretariat.[4]

The NDP's policy-making system differentiated between three types of committees. The first type was the corporate committee, of which there were three: the P&P Board, the Treasury Board, and the Management Board. The second type was the policy committee, of which there were four: Economic Development, Social Policy, Environment Policy, and Justice Policy. Finally, the third type was a business of government committee called the Legislation and Regulations Committee, which was responsible for reviewing all draft legislation and regulations to ensure that they were both technically correct and in accord with government policy.

The NDP's policy-making system was designed to deal with two types of concerns — namely, policy issues and fiscal considerations — and tried to integrate these concerns to the greatest extent possible. The system differentiated between four types of policies to be considered by the cabinet. The first was cabinet-initiated policy, which consisted principally of the strategic priorities set by the cabinet. The second was ministry-initiated policy. Over the life of the government, consideration of policies of this type became progressively subordinated to the cabinet's strategic priorities; nevertheless, a considerable amount of routine policy continued to originate with the line ministries. The third type of policy related to fiscal strategy and allocations; the fourth related to routine government operations.

The P&P Board of the cabinet played the central role in the policy-making process. The consistent effort to impose centralized control over the policy process originated with this committee. The P&P Board set the government's strategic priorities, managed its fiscal plan, and was responsible for integrating the policy priorities into the fiscal plan. The government established and reviewed its strategic priorities semiannually through an iterative process that involved the four policy committees, broad discussion at cabinet retreats, a final confirmation of priorities by the P&P Board, and full cabinet consideration. The full cabinet held formal retreats twice a year, once in September or October and once during the winter, followed by a caucus retreat. At the cabinet retreats there was a periodic review of strategic priorities based on material provided by the policy units of the cabinet office in consultation with the policy staff of the premier's office. The results of that review were confirmed at a special meeting of the P&P Board held after each retreat. Specific initiatives that were designated as strategic priorities were then sent back to the respective policy committees for a further review and returned to the P&P Board and the full cabinet for final approval.

During the first two years of the NDP government the P&P Board also exercised responsibility for the funding of new initiatives; this system ensured a close fit between the approval of strategic priorities and the allocation of new funds to those priorities. The P&P Board reviewed all policy recommendations from the policy committees and the government's fiscal strategy and allocations. In the expenditure management process, the decision-making underlying the budget frequently emerged from joint sessions of the Treasury Board and the P&P Board. These joint sessions were the primary means for integrating policy and fiscal decision-making. The premier chaired the P&P Board and it reported directly to the full cabinet.

The Management Board was responsible for developing human resource policy throughout the public service, conducting collective bargaining with the public service unions, establishing policies for the procurement of goods and services for the government, and maintaining control over the use of information technology in the public sector. Under the NDP, the board was also directed to seek ways to improve the quality of service to the public, promote participatory forms of management, and improve the quality of labour-management relations in the public service.[5]

Treasury Board

One of the NDP government's most significant innovations was to create a separate treasury board as a committee of the cabinet to manage the intense fiscal pressure that it faced. This resulted from the government's dissatisfaction with its initial experience of the fiscal allocation process.

> What was encountered was a financial planning and decision-making system that was fragmented between the Finance Ministry and the Management Board, with the latter responsible for the annual estimates process; weak links between the financial and policy decision-making processes; and an allocation process reflecting years of prosperity that simply added new expenditures without questioning base program expenditures. The new Treasury Board, with the Finance minister as its chair, aimed to resolve the fragmentation in financial decision-making.[6]

The staff of the Treasury Board was formed by combining the planning and estimates division of the Management Board with a large part of what had previously been the Office of the Budget to create the Treasury Board Secretariat. The mandate of the Treasury Board was to manage the fiscal plan for the government, to maintain appropriate spending controls, to manage the annual estimates process, which included regular program reviews of the existing base budgets of line ministries, and to review the fiscal implications of all policy proposals that received approval from the relevant policy committees. The Treasury Board conducted its review of policy initiatives before those initiatives proceeded to the P&P Board to ensure that final policy consideration took full account of fiscal implications.

The government operated with a modified version of an ABX budgeting system. Under this system, the Treasury Board was responsible for the A (base estimates in the budget), while the P&P Board was responsible for the B (new budget initiatives). The P&P Board and the policy committees of the cabinet managed the new initiatives process for the first two fiscal years — 1991–92 and 1992–93 — the only years in which funds had been allocated for new initiatives. Although fiscal pressures severely constrained the amount of money the government could set aside for new initiatives, it felt obligated to fund a certain number that particularly reflected its political priorities. During this period the X (expenditure reducing) budgets were managed by the Corporate Review Committee of Deputy Ministers, whose task was to ensure that reductions were imposed in a manner consistent with government priorities rather than on an across-the-board basis.

In the final three years of the NDP mandate, the expenditure management system changed significantly. Prior to 1993, the dominant view within the government was that its fiscal problems were largely of a cyclical nature and were due to the severity of the recession. Total revenue declined from a peak of $42.9 billion in 1990–91 to $40.8 billion in 1991–92, rising moderately to $41.8 billion in 1992–93 as a result of significant tax increases. At the same time, the deficit grew from a projected surplus prior to the 1990 election to a peak of $12.4 billion in 1992–93. In the middle of planning for the third fiscal year (1993–94) the view that the problem was primarily cyclical in nature was seriously challenged. Early projections indicated that the rate of economic growth and the resulting levels of revenue would not be sufficient to close the deficit gap and that, if immediate action were not taken, the deficit could soar as high as $17 billion.

The dramatic nature of these figures prompted a reassessment of the government's overall fiscal position, leading to the conclusion that it faced a structural gap in its finances. In other words, anticipated rates of economic growth would not, on their own, close the gap between the anticipated level of revenues and the level of public spending. In light of this realization, the nature of the expenditure management process changed dramatically. During initial planning for the third fiscal cycle, the Treasury Board implemented the Multi-Year Expenditure Reduction Plan, which was designed to produce long-term savings by eliminating programs with the lowest priority and slowing expenditure growth. In March and April 1993, this plan was combined with a month-long effort coordinated by the Treasury Board Secretariat and the cabinet office to produce the Expenditure Control Plan. Recommendations emerging from this process were approved at a weekend-long meeting of the full cabinet and all deputy ministers. The combined savings of these plans amounted to $4 billion in the fiscal plan for 1993–94.[7] These savings constituted the third part of the NDP strategy, along with the Social Contract and tax increases, to reduce the projected deficit to under $10 billion. However, the relative collegiality of the expenditure control exercise and its effectiveness were overshadowed by the controversy surrounding the Social Contract.

In addition to creating a separate Treasury Board, another key decision of the NDP in the design of the cabinet committee system was to disband the deputy ministers' "mirror" committees (committees of deputies that replicated the committees of their ministers), which had existed under the Liberal government. Instead, the deputy ministers were made ex officio members of the four cabinet policy committees (Economic Development, Justice Policy, Social Policy and Environment Policy). The justification for this change was the belief that the mirror committees had effectively become the site of policy-making and that ministers were merely rubber-stamping bureaucratic decisions at the cabinet committee level. However, defenders of the mirror system maintained that these committees provided an effective means for resolving design problems in new policy initiatives and for facilitating interministerial coordination, thus allowing ministers to focus on key political issues. In practice, the NDP ministers still insisted on allocating part of their time for "ministers only" meetings, which became a source of some irritation with the deputies. There is little doubt that the NDP's abolition of the mirror committees remained a sore spot for many experienced bureaucrats throughout the government's mandate.

An interesting NDP experiment in the operation of the four policy committees of the cabinet was to appoint chairs who were not members of the P&P Board to afford these committees more independence in their deliberations. In general, this facilitated more free-flowing and open-ended discussions, but the experiment proved short-lived: from early 1993 onwards all chairs of the policy committees were members of the P&P Board. This shift reflected the nature of the policy cycle in the life of a government. In the second half of a mandate the policy process becomes more focused on the upcoming election and consequently more concerned with the government's political agenda. Hence, the decision to make members of the P&P Board the chairs of all of the policy committees reflected the government's desire to concentrate on implementing its previously approved policies. This change increased the influence of the P&P Board members in the overall policy process and was relatively effective in achieving its intended effect.

Central Agencies

What was the role of the central agencies within this system? As noted previously, one of the most significant changes in the NDP redesign of the policy infrastructure was the expansion of the five policy units in the cabinet office (corresponding to the four policy committees and the P&P Board). Policy coordination in the cabinet office was the responsibility of five executive coordinators who reported directly to the deputy secretary to the cabinet. They acted as secretaries to the policy committees and the P&P Board and assisted the chairs of these committees. They also facilitated the flow of policy items from the committees to the P&P Board and communicated the board's directions concerning strategic priorities to the various ministries. Each executive coordinator had a staff of three or four policy advisers. Most of the executive coordinators were career bureaucrats seconded from one of the line ministries; only a few held permanent cabinet office positions.[8] Most stayed for two or three years and then returned to their line ministry jobs. Most also had strong policy backgrounds, as did the policy advisers who worked in their units. Each of these policy advisers served as a window into the cabinet office for one or more of the line ministries. They conveyed the cabinet's directions to the line ministries and other central agencies and monitored the progress of both cabinet and ministry-sponsored initiatives scheduled for consideration by the cabinet policy committees.

Though the policy units played a far less interventionist role than had been expected by many in the party, their creation and subsequent expansion (to between twenty-five and thirty people during the five years of the NDP government) were seen by many in the bureaucracy as a considerable shift in power. Their direct role in managing the government's strategic priorities symbolized an excessive centralization of the policy system in the eyes of public servants who were wedded to the old bureaucratic culture of Queen's Park. Among this latter group there was a strong feeling that the policy-making system had functioned more effectively prior to 1990, when it was more decentralized and deputy ministers enjoyed greater autonomy in the management of their line departments.

The other major central agency, the premier's office, had a policy and issues group consisting of five people. The head of this group functioned as the premier's key policy adviser, while the other four members were responsible for specific policy areas. The policy and issues group was also responsible for ensuring that important policy initiatives received consideration by the NDP caucus immediately before or after they were considered by the P&P Board.

One of the organizational successes of the Rae government was the close working relationship that existed between the premier's office and the cabinet office. The cabinet office policy units were responsible for providing independent and critical policy advice, but once a clear policy direction emerged from the premier's office, their responsibility shifted to working with the line ministries to ensure that policy development proceeded along the desired lines. A close working relationship also existed between the cabinet office and the Treasury Board Secretariat. There was a natural tension between the policy development role of the one agency and the expenditure management role of the other, but both made a consistent effort to ensure coordination. In general, the NDP government's effort to coordinate the activities of the P&P Board, the Treasury Board, and their respective central agencies was highly effective.[9] Whether the policies pursued were the right ones and whether the NDP's fiscal stance was appropriate are, of course, debatable, but organizationally the policy-making system put in place under the NDP demonstrated an ability to produce coordinated outcomes.

The Harris System

It is now appropriate to turn to the new policy-making system put in place by the Harris government since June 1995. The new system and its infrastructure are marked by a number of important changes. The first and most important is the streamlined nature of both the cabinet itself and its decision-making system. The cabinet has been considerably reduced in size compared to its NDP predecessor, in both the number of members and the number of committees. This reduction was facilitated by the new government's agenda — a focus on expenditure reduction and downsizing of the public service requires a policy system that is less elaborate than that required to serve the NDP's broader agenda. The new cabinet consisted of nineteen portfolios and three coordinating committees: the P&P Board, the Management Board, and the Legislation and Regulations Committee. The Treasury Board and its Secretariat were disbanded, and the staff of the latter reallocated to the Ministry of Finance and the Management Board Secretariat, thus effectively restoring the system that existed under the Liberals prior to 1990. The P&P Board is still chaired by the premier, and it still includes the most powerful members of the cabinet.[10]

The tensions between centralizing and decentralizing forces that existed under the NDP and that are endemic in policy-making systems, are quickly re-emerging at the centre of this new system. The structure of cabinet decision-making reveals a strong preference for tight political control by the premier and a small, highly trusted staff in the premier's office. This structure has proved very effective in keeping the cabinet's agenda focused on the government's priorities. Although a number of ad hoc committees have been struck to deal with specific issues, there are no standing committees; this significantly restricts the opportunity for participation in decision-making by ministers on the outer periphery of the cabinet. This is in sharp contrast to the NDP's policy-making system, which encouraged a more collegial style of decision-making within a formal committee structure while trying to maintain the government's control of the overall agenda through the P&P Board and its supporting central agencies. The Conservative system makes less pretence of collegiality and focuses closely on the party's agenda, as laid out in its Common Sense Revolution platform. However, for those policy items that fall outside the ambit of the Common Sense Revolution, individual ministers may still enjoy some latitude.

This clear preference for centralized political control appears to conflict with some changes in the policy infrastructure. The Harris government has, in effect, restored the old order at the bureaucratic level, including appointing strong supporters of the pre-NDP system to key central agency posts. Yet these public servants, who must now work with a highly centralized system, have traditionally favoured a decentralized model. In their view, the system works best when deputy ministers enjoy a substantial degree of autonomy, and as a consequence both the size and role of the policy units in the cabinet office have been significantly reduced. The task of those policy advisers who remain is to support the work of the line ministries; but their discretion in providing policy direction has been narrowly circumscribed. The question thus arises: what will be the eventual effect of these conflicting political and bureaucratic preferences? At a minimum, it may be suggested, the cabinet office might have to revert to a more process-oriented role while the premier's office plays the lead role in substantive policy matters.

If the Conservative policy system is to function efficiently, three potential sources of tension will have to be reconciled. The first is the traditional tension between centralizing and decentralizing pressures. Clearly, the senior bureaucrats who manage the central agencies would prefer a more decentralized policy-making system. One of their early moves was to establish ad hoc committees of deputy ministers whose purpose is to conduct program reviews in key policy areas. These committees roughly overlap with the ministers' ad hoc committees, and it is not clear how the two are linked. The decentralized model of decision-making inherent in the approach of the senior bureaucrats conflicts with the more centralized vision emanating from the premier's office, and the two will need to be reconciled in some manner.

The second source of tension is between the Ministry of Finance and the Management Board Secretariat. The abolition of the Treasury Board and the restoration of the Management Board's responsibility for expenditure management simplify respective roles to some degree. Under the NDP a degree of tension had existed between the fiscal concerns of the Treasury Board and the Management Board's mandate to improve the quality of the public service. The Conservatives' streamlined system subordinates the public sector concerns of the Management Board to the government's fiscal objectives. However, this system also leaves responsibility for major program review with the Ministry of Finance, which creates potential tension between the ministry and the Management Board Secretariat. According to Kaufman:

> ... it could be said that the Conservative Government's central agency reorganization recreates the fragmentation of fiscal planning and management that the former government's Treasury Board reforms aimed to correct. It is tempting to anticipate the reemergence of earlier problems, particularly tensions between Finance and Management Board.[11]

Finally, there remains an underlying potential for conflict between the political and the bureaucratic components of the policy-making system. In addition to the perennial centralization/decentralization dilemma discussed above, there is reason for concern over the central agencies' ability to manage the government's overall policy agenda. In its haste to eliminate features of the NDP's policy system that it found distasteful, the Harris government may have weakened the capacity of the central agencies to facilitate its own policies. Similarly, the disbanding of the cabinet policy committees may mean that ministers no longer have an adequate opportunity to consider the complex issues involved in the scale of expenditure constraint and public service cutbacks that the government is committed to undertaking. Weakening the analytical role of the cabinet office may mean that policy items will arrive at the P&P Board without the prior scrutiny that they require. These deficiencies may result in policy deliberations being inadequately informed and perhaps unnecessarily delayed.

Reports that emerged during the crucial fall term of the Harris government's second year in office indicate that the policy system experienced serious friction when the government shifted from merely reducing expenditures to restructuring the provision of public services at the provincial and municipal levels. Some policy items were arriving in a relatively unfinished state and ministers were forced to send them back for further refinement. The embarassing postponement of the fall (1996) economic statement provided further evidence that the Conservative's policy system was having difficulty responding in a timely fashion to the heavy demands being placed on it. While difficulties during the government's first year may have been nothing more than the teething problems of a new policy system — not unlike those encountered by the NDP during its first year — their persistence well into the second year suggests they may reflect some basic design flaws in the policy system. If this is the case, the Conservatives may be prompted to reconsider some aspects of the former policy system that they abandonned, or they may ultimately be compelled to scale back on the broad scope of their policy agenda.

Endnotes

1. For a broader overview of the political and economic challenges facing the NDP government and its response to them, see Chuck Rachlis and David Wolfe, "An Insider's View of The NDP Government of Ontario: The Politics of Permanent Opposition meets the Economics of Permanent Recession," in

Graham White, ed., *The Government and Politics of Ontario*, 5th ed., Toronto: University of Toronto Press, 1997.

2. See Richard D. French, *How Ottawa Decides: Planning and Industrial Policy-making, 1968–1984*, 2nd ed., Toronto: James Lorimer, 1984; and G. Bruce Doern and Richard Phidd, *Canadian Public Policy: Ideas, Structure, Process*, 2nd ed., Toronto: Nelson, 1992.

3. Peter Aucoin and Herman Bakvis, *The Centralization-Decentralization Conundrum: Organization and Management in the Canadian Government*, Halifax: Institute for Research on Public Policy, 1988.

4. For Bob Rae's views on the transition process and the challenges facing his new government, see *From Protest to Power: Personal Reflections on a Life in Politics*, (Toronto: Viking, 1996), ch. 9.

5. Jay Kaufman, "Program Review in Ontario," in Amelita Armit and Jacques Bourgault, eds., *Hard Choices or No Choices: Assessing Program Review,* Monographs on Canadian Public Administration No. 17, Toronto: Institute of Public Administration of Canada, 1996.

6. Kaufman, "Program Review in Ontario," 95-6.

7. Kaufman, "Program Review in Ontario," 99. For a broader discussion of the Expenditure Control Plan in the context of the government's attempt to implement a social contract, see also Lawrence J. Hanson, "From a Contracting Economy to the Social Contract: Governing Recessionary Ontario." Paper presented to the annual meeting of the Canadian Political Science Association, Brock University, St. Catherines, Ontario, June, 1996.

8. For the first three years of the NDP government, the author served as the executive coordinator for economic and labour policy, which undoubtedly influences this account. He was one of the few cabinet office staff seconded from outside the public service. After two and a half years, the position of executive coordinator for the P&P Board was left vacant and the policy advisers in this unit reported directly to the deputy secretary.

9. This view is also expressed by Jay Kaufman, the former secretary to the Treasury Board and deputy minister of Finance (Kaufman, "Program Review in Ontario").

10. Richard Loreto, "Common Sense or Revolution: The New Cabinet System in Ontario," *Public Sector Management* 6:4 (1995): 6–7.

11. Kaufman, "Program Review in Ontario," 99–100.

Further Reading

Blizzard, Christina. *Right Turn: How the Tories Took Ontario.* Toronto: Dundurn, 1995.

Erhing, George, and Wayne Roberts. *Giving Away a Miracle: Lost Dreams, Broken Promises and the Ontario NDP.* Oakville: Mosaic Press, 1993.

Gagnon, Georgette, and Dan Rath. *Not Without Cause: David Peterson's Fall from Grace.* Toronto: HarperCollins, 1991.

Hoy, Claire. *Bill Davis.* Toronto: Methuen, 1985.

Monanhan, Patrick. *Storming the Pink Palace: Bob Rae, the NDP and the Crisis of the Canadian Left.* Toronto: Lester, 1995.

Progressive Conservative Party of Ontario. *The Common Sense Revolution* Toronto, 1994.

Rae, Bob. *From Protest to Power: Personal Reflections on a Life in Politics.* Toronto: Viking, 1996.

Speirs, Rosemary. *Out of The Blue: The Fall of the Tory Dynasty in Ontario.* Toronto: Macmillan,1986.

Walkom, Thomas. *Rae Days: The Rise and Follies of the NDP.* Toronto: Key Porter, 1994.

White, Graham, ed. *The Government and Politics of Ontario,* 5th ed. Toronto: University of Toronto Press, 1997.

Contributors

Peter Dungan is Associate Director of the Policy and Economic Analysis Program (PEAP) at the University of Toronto and Adjunct Associate Professor of Economics. In his work with PEAP, Professor Dungan has been closely involved with the construction and application of macroeconomic models of the Canadian and Ontario economies.

Geoffrey E. Hale holds a Ph.D. in Political Science from the University of Western Ontario, specializing in Canadian Politics and Public Policy. He has worked for the Government of Ontario on the restructuring of the agency sector. His current research is on labour and workplace policies.

Robert MacDermid is Associate Professor of Political Science at York University. His research interests include elections and electoral behaviour, and he is currently completing a research project on television advertising by Canadian political parties.

Sid Noel, the editor of this volume, is Professor of Political Science at the University of Western Ontario. Among his recent publications are *Patrons, Clients, Brokers* (1990), a study of the origins of Ontario politics, and articles and chapters of books on political patronage, Canadian political parties, and the Ontario political culture.

A. Brian Tanguay is Associate Professor of Political Science at Wilfrid Laurier University. He is co-editor (with Alain-G. Gagnon) of *Democracy With Justice: Essays in Honour of Khayyam Zev Paltiel* (1992) and *Canadian Parties in Transition* (2nd ed., 1996). He has published articles on labour relations and party politics in Quebec, social democracy in Canada, and the role of interest groups in the political process.

Graham White is Professor of Political Science at the University of Toronto. He has written widely on Canadian provincial government and on the politics of the Northwest Territories. Among his books are *The Ontario Legislature: A Political Analysis* (1989), *Northern*

Governments in Transition (1995), and *The Government and Politics of Ontario* (5th ed., 1997). For several years he served as Director of the Ontario Legislature Internship Programme.

John Wilson is Professor of Political Science at the University of Waterloo, where he has been teaching Canadian politics since 1964. He is the author of several articles on the nature of Ontario politics and the party system and voting behaviour of the province.

David A. Wolfe is Associate Professor of Political Science at the University of Toronto in Mississauga. He is the author of numerous articles on economic policy making in Canada and Ontario. From 1990 to 1993, he served as the Executive Coordinator for Economic and Labour Policy in the Cabinet Office, Government of Ontario.

Peter Woolstencroft is Associate professor of Political Science and Associate Dean of Arts at the University of Waterloo. He has published articles on parties and elections in Canada, electoral geography, education policy, methods of selecting party leaders, and spatial aspects of urban politics.

Index

PRINTED AND BOUND
IN BOUCHERVILLE, QUÉBEC, CANADA
BY MARC VEILLEUX IMPRIMEUR INC.
IN AUGUST, 1997